Devoted Parent

Devotions from Christian Teachers to Parents

Dedication

Dear Parents,

We share your passion: your children.

The spirit of this devotion book is to speak heart to heart about raising children. We want to encourage and affirm you in your role as parents, as well as share a little of what the Lord has taught us as we carry out the joyful responsibility of teaching your children. So often, as we are teaching them, we are blessed to catch glimpses of what can be only your influence. Those moments are a blessing to us. They show us how to teach each child better.

Dedicated to parents and educators everywhere who sacrifice so much for the sake of children.

Our true confession is that sometimes we wish there were more opportunities to partner with you. We thought, perhaps a devotional would be a loving place to share our hearts.

We want to overcome what we see as a growing hurdle. Though our society is dedicated to providing education for all, that very provision has sometimes encouraged parents to seemingly "drop the child at the schoolhouse door." With new school procedures that limit parent physical access, we know parents may even feel unwelcome in the educational process. Nothing could be farther from the truth. We need you.

The Lord gifted you with your children, and no one understands their hearts better. We desire to teach them, but only as a secondary partner to you, the parent. Our desire is to be the favorite tool in your teaching toolbox as you "bring up a child in the way that he should go" (Proverbs 22:6, NKJV).

This devotional is written to bring our heart to yours; never hesitate to bring your heart to us.

In partnership,

The Administration and Faculty
SUMMIT CHRISTIAN ACADEMY
Email us your comments at <u>devotedparent@sca-kc.org</u>.

Table of Contents

Introduction
5

Courageous Parenting
7

Creative Parenting
103

Faithful Parenting
23

Loving Parenting
123

Joyful Parenting
45

Humble Parenting
143

Thankful Parenting
65

Wise Parenting
161

Grace-filled Parenting
85

Patient Parenting
181

Introduction

This book was written as a labor of love from a single faculty. All proceeds from its sale will help underwrite the cost of a child's education that integrates a Christian worldview and daily Bible study.

Each of these readings was written by an educator. Every author was provided a general format and asked to write as the Holy Spirit directed and in his own style. We hope you find a favorite! You may notice some devotions are deliberately anonymous. Anonymity may have been chosen by the writer or the editor. In addition, different translations of Scripture were used and reflect the personal choices of the authors.

This book may be used as either a reference or as a devotional.

As a reference, we recognize that there are times of joy as well as times of tears within the seasons of parenting. For example, should life bring about a season of fear, you may wish to read several devotions on courageous parenting. Or, as you celebrate your child's choice to follow Jesus, you may want to spend time in the section on joyful parenting. Our hope is that this book can be an encouragement for you time and again.

As a devotional, it is written to be read Monday through Friday during the school year. It encompasses a typical number of school days from August to May. Each month shares a devotion to encourage a spiritual virtue within you as a parent.

Each division ends with a place to write your reflections meant to encourage you the next time you pick up the book.

Courageous Parenting

Have I not commanded you? Be strong and courageous.
Do not be afraid; do not be discouraged, for the LORD
your God will be with you wherever you go.

Joshua 1:9, NIV

Clay Pots I

For God, who said, "Let there be light in the darkness," has made this light shine in our hearts so we could know the glory of God that is seen in the face of Jesus Christ. We now have this light shining in our hearts, but we ourselves are like fragile clay jars containing this great treasure.

II Corinthians 4:6-7, NLT

~

God has given us the indescribable treasure of His nature, power, and glory. Somehow these flawed clay pots we inhabit are enabled to deliver streams of living water to a sin-darkened desert. We are filled up, poured out, and filled up again.

His light shines most effectively when our clay pots are cracked, chipped and sometimes… shattered into a million pieces. We make jokes about being "cracked pots," but submitting to the Potter's wheel is uncomfortable, even painful.

> ## Submitting to the Potter's wheel is uncomfortable.

It's hard enough when we are the ones spinning on the Potter's wheel, but when God allows our children to experience the pressure that creates cracks, the pain that chips and breaks, and those awful heartaches that threaten to shatter their lives and ours, well, trusting God gets taken to a whole new level. I've had so many wrestling matches with God over this; you'd think I was auditioning for a televised smack down! If you need someone in your corner to tag for a few rounds, call me.

Being molded isn't easy, but watching our children go through the process can be even more painful. In those moments, we need to trust the Potter's hands.

Father, when I dedicated this precious child to you, it seemed like the obvious decision, but now? I know you understand how much this hurts. You lived the heartbreak of watching Your Son suffer and die for me and for my children. I don't know how to walk this path with them. Show us together how to draw comfort, grace, wisdom, and strength from You and from Your people.

~ Grandma Ruth

Just Stand

And he said, "Listen all Judah and the inhabitants of Jerusalem and King Jehoshaphat: thus says the Lord to you, 'Do not fear or be dismayed because of this great multitude, for the battle is not yours but God's. You need not fight in this battle; station yourselves, stand and see the salvation of the Lord on your behalf, O Judah and Jerusalem.' Do not fear or be dismayed; tomorrow go out to face them, for the Lord is with you."

I Chronicles 20: 15 & 17, NASB

~

I love this story! Jehoshaphat was faced with an impossible situation. He knew he did not have the strength or the resources to be victorious in this inevitable battle. I am inspired by his response: he cried out to God in honesty. He was afraid and did not know what to do, but his eyes were on Him. The prophet spoke the above words of hope to Jehoshaphat, and Jehoshaphat obeyed. God did completely deliver His people…and then some!! All Jehoshaphat had to do was stand and watch God be God.

So many times in our spiritual walk, we are faced with impossible situations. Too often, we immediately begin trying to figure out how we can manage it in our own ability, eliminating the opportunity to experience God's magnificent power in our lives. Sometimes, He asks us to take action and equips us for the job. But how exciting it is when He wants us to let Him do the fighting for us, and all we have to do is just stand!

Stand and watch God be God.

God, we know that even in our parenting, we will face situations that are out of our control. Remind us, Father, to boldly cry out to You in those times and confess our inadequacy. Strengthen us with Your power; and if need be, get us out of the way so that You can work mightily for us.

~ Trissa Lucht, choir teacher

Allowing Time

How often I wanted to gather your children together, as a hen gathers
her brood under her wings, but you were not willing!

Luke 13:34b, NKJV

~

Good families lead full lives: full of the need to's (laundry/lawn), the want to's (hair dyes/night with the guys), and the guilted to's (volunteer/ask relatives here). With the brief 24-hour day, too often we race by the priority. Most parents would agree that next to their relationship with the Lord and with each other, their children are what make life worth living.

Life is meant to pulse us into the arms of one another.

It doesn't matter that they're typically sticky, frequently exhausting, and incredibly demanding. Our eyes fall on them in the rush, and we experience the heart of God. Throughout Scripture we are admonished as His children to pause and know our Father. This is the model we must take with our own parenting. The pound of life isn't meant to distract us from the moments of heart binding. Rather, life is meant to pulse us into the arms of one another, leaving the world behind.

The extra hour spent rocking the baby, the silly time on the floor playing dolls and fire trucks, the conversation around the kitchen table after eating and before dishes are done—these are the ethereal moments that can drift by without capture, if we are not careful.

As we are God's children, He wants to know our hearts. In the spirit of modeling that truth, it is okay to stop the rush in order to learn your child's heart. For in that moment, you are demonstrating their heavenly Father's own longing to know them.

Dear Lord, My heart is to serve You completely. Sometimes in my rush to do the right things, I confess, I don't do the most important things. My ideas of priorities keep getting in the way. Lord, right now, I confess this as sin. I ask that Your sweet Holy Spirit whisper to my heart every time the busyness creeps in to snatch the time meant for my children. Let Your mind become my mind. Father, help us as a family cling to one another and truly know each other's hearts.

~ Kimberlee Gill, academic dean

Being Bold

The Spirit of God, who raised Jesus from the dead, lives in you.

Romans 8:11a, NLT

~

Did you read that? I don't know if you caught that middle part, but Paul is talking about the same Spirit that raised our Savior from the grave! That is what lives inside of you. This is a power that cannot be measured, and yet there are so many Christians that live without utilizing this power.

In Romans 8, Paul is talking about the role of the Holy Spirit in our salvation. Paul walks us through it: we are not condemned because we belong to Jesus. Because we belong to Him we have been given the gift of the Holy Spirit. And because we have the Spirit, we are freed from sin and death. That is kind of a big deal. We were given this amazing powerful gift to be free, yes, but also to use this power in our lives. We are called by God to live like Jesus lived. Jesus lived such a radical life. How are we to live this life radically as Jesus did without using our biggest tool, the Spirit?

> You are your child's best shot at learning how to live.

As a teacher I see so many students who do not know what it means to live radically. They don't even know they are supposed to live like Jesus. I know many of them do not even realize they have the Spirit living in them. This absence of understanding is a tragedy and an injustice to my students. That is why I believe it is so important that I do my best to live like Jesus as an example to them. However, who is more of an example to these students than their parents? Nobody!

Parents, you are your child's best shot at learning how to live with the power that we have in Christ. They need you, and they do not even know it! They need you to show them how to be bold by living differently than the rest of the world as Jesus did. They need to be shown the radical life they can lead and the amazing things they can accomplish through the power of the Holy Spirit.

Dear Heavenly Father, Please help me to be bold today. May You give me the courage to live, not according to my own strength, but by the power You have gifted me. I pray You help me to be an example to my child as Jesus was an example to me. In Your Son's name I pray, Amen.

~ Mrs. LaFollette, secondary math

Rough Start

*He replied, "Because you have so little faith. Truly I tell you, if you have faith
as small as a mustard seed, you can say to this mountain, 'Move from here
to there,' and it will move. Nothing will be impossible for you."*

Matthew 17:20, NIV

~

I have entrusted my precious grandchild to God's care. While lying in bed,
weeping and praying over the future of the love and joy of my heart, my
grandson, it occurs to me that others might not see him as I do. He came to me
beaten and battered, not physically, but emotionally and spiritually. My eyes
light up as I see the man he is becoming. But, others may see him differently.
He struggles while using his tongue instead of his brain; he does not trust
what most adults say. His teachers want to make sure I know he has missing
assignments and that his research paper needs a lot of work. I want them to know he has a tender heart and that Jesus has such awesome plans for his life.

Jesus has not given up on you or your child. Nothing is impossible for the Lord we serve.

Perhaps your child has a future that appears less than favorable by others. Maybe your child's transition to school has been difficult. Do not give up or be discouraged! Each precious child is important in the kingdom of God. Jesus has not given up on you or your child. Nothing is impossible for the Lord we serve.

Take courage. Our faith can move mountains.

*Father God, Thank You for this child that You have put in my life. Though he struggles
and often gives up too easily, he is a work in process. The man he is becoming is
directed by You and those that You have cross his path. I ask that others see him as You
do, even though he is not quite there yet. Amen.*

~ A prayin', educatin' grandma

Fearful Parenting

To this end also we pray for you always, that our God will count you worthy of your calling, and fulfill every desire for goodness and the work of faith with power, so that the name of our Lord Jesus will be glorified in you, and you in Him, according to the grace of our God and the Lord Jesus Christ.

II Thessalonians 1:11-12, NASB

~

We all have the propensity to parent out of fear. Fear of what others will think of me. Fear of what others will think of my children. Fear of discipline, and either pushing my child away, or getting caught and in trouble. Fear of failing altogether. I know I have been down this road, and it is not a pretty drive.

However, I take great encouragement from a couple of simple truths that I believe God intentionally allowed to be planted in my heart at pivotal moments in my parenting. First of all, God divinely appointed me to be the mother to my three children. This divine appointment means not by accident or by coincidence. God in His just love and mercy chose me to care for these children on earth. He does require me to hold them with palms up and open. I cannot cling to my children or try to make them mine; they really are His. He created them; He gave them a hope and a purpose. My job is to be the mother He has called me to be one season at a time.

God continues to equip me.

The second truth is this: God continues to equip me to be the parent He has called me to be. This process is never over, because as my children grow, so must I. I will never have all the answers, but He leads me in to find them. I have also found that He always provides wisdom from parents who are one step ahead of me. Yet, even as I am careful whom I glean from, I will still mess up. Thankfully, God's grace is sufficient, and His mercies are new every morning!

Father God, Thank You for giving me the privilege of mothering my children. I thank You for all that I learn about You and Your love and mercy through parenting. I pray for every parent reading this, that fear would be removed and replaced with confidence in Your divine appointment. Lord, may You be glorified in our parenting. Amen

~ Trish Teilborg, elementary teacher

Let Us Dance!

*You turned my wailing into dancing; you removed my sackcloth and
clothed me with joy, that my heart may sing your praises and not be silent.
LORD my God, I will praise you forever.*

Psalm 30:11-12

~

In 2 Samuel 6, David danced as an expression of joy and gratitude to the Lord
on the occasion of the return of the Ark of the Covenant to Jerusalem. His
wife Michal, daughter of Saul, was watching from a window and despised him
in her heart. She reproached him for how he had lowered himself as a king
before the people. But David's heart was pure. David said to Michal: "I was
celebrating before the LORD… I am willing to shame and humiliate myself
even more than this!"

The story ends with a sad report saying that Michal after this had no child until
the day of her death. She was cursed at that instant. In her mind, David was
making a fool of himself. David was dancing before God with all his might and
did not care what others thought about him.

> **What we
> choose ... will
> decide our
> blessing or
> our curse.**

There is so much to learn from the simplicity of this
story. We are living in a world that is constantly
changing and dictating to us how we need to act,
speak, behave and even perform under different
circumstances. But what we choose to do in each
situation will decide our blessing or our curse.
Michal decided to watch and criticize. David chose
the best part, doing exactly what pleased God's
heart. He understood that it was more important to
be a pleasing sacrifice before the eyes of the Lord,
regardless of how foolish he looked in front of his kingdom or to his wife.

Sometimes we need to throw off the world's chains and dance before Him
like no one is looking. Today, I will decide to please Him and dance over my
circumstances, and I will rejoice in the Lord with all my heart and strength. He
is faithful and deserves all the glory and all our praise! Let us rejoice and dance
before Him!

*Lord, Open the eyes of my heart so I can know You more and please You through any
circumstance. Let me seek you and honor You with my praise and exalt Your name
above everything. I want to rejoice in You and experience Your peace. Remove any
thought or fear within me that could hold me back from being who You want me to be.
You are the strength of my life; whom should I fear?*

~ I. Velázquez, artist

Never Alone

No one will be able to stand against you all the days of your life. As I was with Moses, so I will be with you; I will never leave you nor forsake you.

Joshua 1:5b, NIV

~

I was on my first ski trip shortly after I graduated from college. I had gone early with some friends who were experienced skiers. We were waiting on the rest of our group from church to arrive by bus. I was nervous about taking ski lessons, but knew I would have the comfort of other "first time friends" taking the class with me. As we were waiting, we found out the bus had mechanical trouble and would not be arriving until later that night. That meant I was headed to ski lessons alone! My friends had grown up skiing, so they headed off to the slopes and wished me well in my lesson. I stood frozen, not thinking I could do it, when I heard familiar words running through my head…"I will never leave you nor forsake you…I will never leave you nor forsake you…" I can still picture where I was standing and the steps forward I took as I let those words ring through my head.

A beginner ski lesson might not seem like a mountain-moving moment, but those words from the Lord became words I have clung to through many other situations that have come my way. I have heard those words as I started a new job, I have heard them as I got off the plane alone in a third-world country, and I have heard those words as I stood at the cemetery after my mom's funeral. In all of those situations, my flesh told me, "I cannot do this!" and then His words would softly come, "I will never leave you nor forsake you… I will never leave you nor forsake you."

He has promised never to leave us.

We are reminded of this promise in several different places in the Bible, but I especially like the reference to it in the book of Joshua because it says "As I was with Moses, so I will be with you." I've always loved the reminder that He's with me just like He was with the amazing prophet Moses.

Let those words ring through your head the next time you feel alone and feel like you cannot face the steps ahead of you. He has promised NEVER to leave us!

Dear Heavenly Father, Thank You for Your promise to never leave us nor forsake us. Thank You for the countless times You have reminded me of that and forgive me for the times I tried to do it alone. Help us all to keep our focus on You. Give us Your strength in the hard times and let us praise You through them and on the other side!

~ Julie Ray, first grade teacher

The Journey

Be strong and courageous. Do not fear or be in dread of them, for it is the Lord your God who goes with you. He will not leave you or forsake you.

Deuteronomy 31:6, RSV

~

Sitting on a lawn chair waiting to view the Fourth of July fireworks with my family, I gazed at the beautiful night sky. It was such a testimony of God's greatness. How blessed I was to have the same amazing God caring for me, my children, and my grandchildren. His presence has been especially important considering these last few years in my life.

He is there to provide strength and courage.

Within a period of six years, I lost my husband and best friend of twenty-seven years; and I was diagnosed first with colon cancer followed two years later with breast cancer. The school where I had taught middle school for many years closed, requiring a new resume and job interviews. What was God trying to teach me? Where was He leading? What was going to be the end result of all the suffering?

God has taught me a most important lesson through it all. It is not about experiencing the destination; it is the journey we do not want to miss. Along any path He takes us, I can testify, He is there to provide strength and courage. He is faithfully keeping His promises day by day. He is blessing us with the experience of His sweet presence all along the way. What a tragedy it would be to miss such blessings because we are trying to figure out the "why's?" or "when's?" or "where's?"

My prayer is for my children, grandchildren, and others I know to see the value the journey has become in my life because I am traveling it with Jesus.

Lord, Help me to fully experience the joy of the journey with You by my side.

~ **Donna Ambro, junior high teacher and mother of two beautiful daughters**

All Things

His divine power has granted to us all things that pertain to life and godliness,
through the knowledge of him who called us to his own glory and excellence,
by which he has granted to us his precious and very great promises, so that
through them you may become partakers of the divine nature, having escaped
from the corruption that is in the world because of sinful desire.

II Peter 1:3-4, ESV

~

It is a Monday morning. I left my home in a state of disarray with an empty fridge and many loads of laundry still to conquer. In my classroom, stacks of papers, lesson plans and files litter my desk and remind me that I am behind. Students with conflicts, difficulties and various life obstacles burden my heart and distract my thinking. Twenty middle school students bounce around my classroom before the bell rings, and our week will commence. I have no idea how my hastily prepared lesson will play out, and I am not sure I have the energy to fill in the lesson's gaps with sheer enthusiasm and exuberance. I am so tired.

He tells me I have everything I need.

Usually, this is when the pity-party sets in and I begin composing a list of what I need in order for this day to go well. "If I just had…" and the listing begins: more time, a better classroom, more resources, a day off, a maid, etc…. Sometimes, in the midst of these overwhelmed moments, the above verse will light up in my memory and set my heart free. It does not matter what surrounds me and what I think I need! I have been promised with "precious and very great promises" that I have everything I need when it comes to "life and godliness." Everything I need is found in knowing Jesus! He is shepherd, He is king, He is priest, He is redeemer, He is holy, He is conqueror… and He tells me I have everything I need. It almost makes me laugh, in the midst of the daunting reality that is Monday morning. The One who spoke this wild world into existence is with me in this moment, using His power to give me "all things" that have to do with this life. Let Monday do its worst! Christ is ablaze in my heart, equipping me in ways I cannot imagine. I have everything I need.

Heavenly Father, You are so generous to us! You not only save us from the death and horrors of sin, but You equip us for every obstacle that our varied and cluttered lives throw our way. Oh, how I long to know Jesus more! Teach me Your promises! May they appear precious. May they appear enormously great. You are kind to us always. May the way we conquer this day show that we believe and treasure Your promise to give us all things.

~ A middle school teacher

That Boy

All who rage against you will surely be ashamed and disgraced; those who oppose you will be as nothing and perish. Though you search for your enemies, you will not find them. Those who wage war against you will be as nothing at all. For I am the Lord your God who takes hold of your right hand and says to you, Do not fear; I will help you.

Isaiah 41:11-13, NIV

~

He's that boy. The one that falls through the cracks. The one that endures the snide remarks that are made behind the teacher's back. The one that has two hours of homework every night. The one that is short for his age. The one that has medication that causes him to have twitches. The one that is picked last in PE and never has a partner for projects. The one that sits alone at lunch. The one that longs to belong but does not. He is THAT boy.

Stand firm ... allow God to work.

How does God see that boy? He's unique, full of love, and willing to help those in need. He is the one that has strength and courage. He is the one that includes others that need friends. He is the one that reaches out to younger children and tries to mentor them. He is the one who will reach others for Christ due to his great social ability and charm. He is the one that the teacher can trust to tell the truth. He is the one that will grow up and be on time for work due to his strong work ethic. God says...he is THAT boy.

How do you give a child strength who is being picked on or even bullied? Coming from a mother who has personally been through this...it is not always an easy task. Christ experienced it personally on the cross when He died for our sins. People hurled insults at Him, mocked Him, and He was tortured. He could have called 10,000 angels, but He chose rather to die for you and for me.

As a parent of a child going through this, remind them of the Truth. The Lord has called us to be courageous and to forgive those who persecute us. By His grace, we are overcomers.

There will be many tears, and there will be times when Mama Bear wants to rush out to defend her cub. Remember to bring the situation back to Christ. Stand firm on the Scripture and allow God to work.

Dear Lord, You know everything. You know our hurts and our pain. I pray for peace and protection for our kids. Keep the enemy away. Help our kids to build each other up with love and encouragement. Thank You for blessing me with a son that is strong enough to be "that boy."

~ An educating mom

The Sonshine

I can do all things through Christ who strengthens me.

Philippians 4:13, NKJV

~

It was one of the first sun-filled, lazy days of summer break for this teacher, and I was delighting in the thought of spending the summer months enjoying uninterrupted time with my toddler.

This particular day my daughter was playing in the living room while I prepared a crisp summer salad for the evening meal. I peeked around the corner into the room to check on her activities. The sun was stretching long rays of light through the windows across the living room. Amber was lifting her tiny legs and trying to sit on the rays of light. She was becoming increasingly frustrated with her inability to mount the inviting beams. It was comical as she tried again and again only to fall on the floor.

That memorable scene was almost thirty years ago, but it is forever etched in the heart and mind of this mother. I remember realizing that day how innocent and impressionable my little one was as she thought riding the sun's rays was something she could accomplish.

All things are possible with God.

God has blessed me with two beautiful daughters since that day, and I have prayed many times that the Lord would protect them and give them wisdom beyond their years. I also prayed that He would give them the mindset that all things are possible with God (Matthew 19:26, ESV).

Lord, Thank You for protecting the hearts and minds of my children. Thank You for giving them the confidence and wisdom that only comes from You.

~ Donna Ambro, mother and teacher

Raising Overcomers

So do not fear, for I am with you; do not be dismayed, for I am your God. I will strengthen you and help you; I will uphold you with my righteous right hand.

Isaiah 41:10, NIV

~

We like to think that our children listen to what we say and learn from lessons we have tried to teach them, but the truth is our children will learn more from our actions than our words. It is so important that the words we speak to our children match the actions we live on a daily basis. As much as we would like to think that we can protect and shield our children from hurt, it is just not always possible. Your child is going to be faced with struggles, heartaches, and ups and downs many times in life. It is inevitable. Yet, you have the ability to embed the hope and faith within them that they will need to overcome their battles.

You have the ability to embed the hope and faith within them.

Our children learn from example; so if they see us broken and defeated when faced with difficulties, that is the behavior they will mimic when tough times fall upon them. Now, on the other hand, if they see us putting all of our faith in the Lord and truly trusting in Him, then we are teaching our children to believe in their hearts that the Lord will help them through any and all struggles that come before them. We must do more than speak the words to trust in the Lord; we must show our children that we will stay strong through the storms of our life and know that God has planned sunny days ahead of us.

One of the most precious gifts we can give our children is to instill in them the power to become overcomers by living a life led by faith and not by fear. Remind your children every day that they can overcome any obstacle when they trust in the Lord our Savior!

Dear Lord, I come to You with an open heart and open mind. You know my heart, and I know You can read my every thought. Please Lord help me to lead by example even through the toughest times. Work through me to help teach my children to trust in You with all of their hearts. I know there will be times my children will be faced with challenges, and my prayer to You is that You will strengthen them through every obstacle so they may overcome. Please wrap Your arms around my family and help me to teach my children to walk by faith. In Jesus' name I pray, Amen.

~ An overcomer

Rough Roads

"For I know the plans I have for you," declares the Lord, "plans to prosper you and not to harm you, plans to give you a hope and a future. Then you will call on me and come and pray to me, and I will listen to you. You will seek me and find me when you seek me with all your heart."

Jeremiah 29:11-13, NIV

~

Go...Stop...Merge...No Crossing...Yield...Construction Zone Ahead...Rest Stop....road signs, yes. These are also signs that God places in our lives on a daily basis.

As a young child, I had one dream--to be married and to have children, one boy and one girl. While my other friends were pretending to be doctors, teachers, and singers, I just wanted to be a mommy and a wife. God did grant me my wish, but my journey as a mom and a wife would be full of unanticipated road signs.

> My journey as a mom and a wife would be full of unanticipated road signs.

GO...When I met my husband at college, God had me leave my hometown and move to another state. I did so without any question in my mind. It was easy; I was in love.

MERGE...I soon realized that the merging of his family and my family would not be smooth. There were many trials in this area of our life.

YIELD...Loss of work, financial struggles and my son's struggles with his education forced me to wait for God's next step in our lives. It always felt like it was one step forward and two steps back.

CONSTRUCTION ZONE...This may have been the hardest road sign for me personally. The family that I had dreamed of and prayed for was crumbling. The breakdown of our marriage and family structure was headed for a divorce.

REST STOP AHEAD...This sign in my life actually proved to be the hardest, yet most valuable. In the moment of my life where I felt defeated and about to give up, I heard God tell me to be patient and in Him I would find rest. Was it that simple?

continued

God had a plan for my life as that little girl. He never promised it would be a princess world, but He did promise that if I trusted in Him that He would direct my path.

Dear Lord, Thank You for the twists and turns in my life that continue leading me to You. In those times of trouble, You have given me strength and encouragement. Help me to always make good decisions in the way I react to the detour signs that You place in my life. Thank You for listening to the desire of my five-year-old heart and blessing me with the perfect family for me.

~ A teacher in the midst of life's journey

Faithful Parenting

Moreover it is required in stewards
that a man be found faithful.

I Corinthians 4:2, KJV

Faith Walking

For we live by faith, not by sight.

II Corinthians 5:7, NIV

~

Two years ago I gave a group of 15 to 20-year-olds a challenge, "Go where God is telling you." This would seem basic and generic if you did not realize that we were in a room preparing for a ten-day journey as part of a leadership/mission trip. They were given vans, money for food, and drivers for the journey. They stared at me, waiting for the punch line. I left the room, and they stared at each other.

God wants us to live, with full reliance on Him.

We live this every day. We know that God has a plan and a direction for us, but so often we want the full itinerary. We want pictures, charts, liability plans, and a clause that allows us to get out of this contract if something comes up. This was not how Christ worked. Excuses were not allowed, plans were not given, and the future always seemed to be in doubt. I wonder if that is how God wants us to live: with full reliance on Him.

I always wondered how this challenge would have worked with adults. Would someone have tried to take charge? How long would it have taken the group to come up with a plan?

I was so proud of our group. They prayed…they voted…they prayed again… they voted again, then changed their minds because the location they voted on was not where they felt God wanted them to go. We left…not really knowing what we were going to do, or where we were staying. God opened doors. We served, and God moved in our hearts. I want to live life this way.

Dear Lord, Give me enough light to see the next step, and yet do not give me the whole picture, so I can learn to trust You with my future.

~ Wayne Stam, Bible teacher

It Grew!

Abraham was almost a hundred years old, much past the age for having children, and Sarah could not have children. Abraham thought about all this, but his faith in God did not become weak. He never doubted that God would keep his promise, and he never stopped believing. He grew stronger in his faith and gave praise to God. Abraham felt sure that God was able to do what he had promised.

Romans 4:19-21, NCV

~

I am not much of a gardener, but I do enjoy planting a few things and watching them grow and bloom. It is funny how tickled I get at each stage of a flower's growth. It is just so fascinating and pleasing that that plant, functioning within God's divine design, does it all on its own! In contrast, I am always puzzled and saddened when a plant, which bloomed so beautifully one year ago, does not develop or even seems diseased. What happened? Why did this plant grow so big and beautiful last year but not this year? Was it the weather? Was there something "in the air"? I never come up with a satisfying answer to my queries, but I do not give up the faith. I have lived in my current home long enough to know that this scenario will happen every year. Somewhere in my yard, something will not bloom. Nevertheless, it does flourish the next season.

Are you, a family member or a friend not "blooming" in this season? Keep the faith! Just like me, the amateur gardener, you will question the "whys." Just like Abraham you will "think about all this." His faith in God, however, did not become weak. He never doubted God and never stopped believing. He grew stronger in his faith and gave praise to God. Oh, did I mention that when my "dead" plants return the next season, they are always bigger and healthier than before. Praise God!

> **Never stop believing— growing stronger in our faith.**

Dear Jesus, Thank you for the times in our lives when we seem to flourish and for the times when we seem dormant. Encourage us to look to biblical patriarchs like Abraham and to never doubt, to never stop believing—to continue growing stronger in our faith, praising God all the way! In Jesus' name, Amen.

~ Mrs. @, Who likes to play "gardener" ☺

God's Virtues

Hear, O Israel: The Lord our God, the Lord is one! You shall love the Lord your God with all your heart, with all your soul, and with all your strength. And these words which I command you today shall be in your heart. You shall teach them diligently to your children, and shall talk of them when you sit in your house, when you walk by the way, when you lie down, and when you rise up.

Deuteronomy 6:4-7, NKJV

~

Teach your child how to think morally.

The world's morality seems to come in all shapes and sizes. Yet Christian parents should measure their values exclusively against the standards of God's Word. Virtues originate with God and reflect the person of Christ. As with Jesus, they are the same yesterday, today and tomorrow. Our virtue then defines our morality.

The moral mandate God has set for us requires us to focus on the value of others. In stark contrast to the current thinking of society, we need to teach our children to consider others before themselves.

In Deuteronomy 6, Moses had an incredible task in dealing with hundreds of thousands of Israelites who left Egypt with twisted values and no moral compass. In verses 4-6, he told the parents of Israel three principles of moral instruction that still apply to our lives today.

First, unlike what the Egyptians believed, there is only one God to please. God is morally perfect and all biblical virtue is an extension of His character. We must not base our morality on society's values, but on biblical values.

Second, moral training begins with the parents. Before you teach your children, Moses said, "These words shall be in your hearts." If the principles of moral conduct are not embedded in your heart, you cannot pass them on to your children.

Third, moral training is to take place during normal day-to-day activities. Take advantage of those times of non-conflict to teach your child how to think morally. We cannot teach them only what to do, but we must also teach them why they should do it. Giving them the moral reason why allows them to internalize virtues.

continued

26

Dear Lord, I submit myself to You. Help me to walk in righteousness and virtue so that I can train my children how to think and act morally. Give me the communication, teaching and nurturing skills that I must have. Give me direction and shed light on opportunities to embed Your virtues on my child's heart. Thank You, Lord, for these precious children that You have entrusted to my care.

~ Teacher

Childlike Prayers

Do not be anxious about anything, but in everything, by prayer and supplication with thanksgiving let your requests be made known to God.

Philippians 4:6, ESV

~

As a first grade teacher in a Christian school, I have the joy of daily hearing children present their requests to God through prayer. They ask God for things they want to see happen, for friends and family they want to be healed, for the needs of fellow classmates, and sometimes they so sweetly pray for their teacher. It is the innocence of their prayers that makes them so endearing to my heart, sometimes bringing tears to my eyes, as they fully expect Him to answer them.

Fully expect Him to answer.

I also never lack for a volunteer to pray for the class. They are eager to do it. I wonder what happens to our eagerness to pray as we get older, especially in public. I think we begin to doubt that our prayers might not be good enough compared to others who might be listening, or maybe we think He just will not answer them. What we need to remember is that our audience is not those around us, but it is the ever-listening ears of our Heavenly Father. He is certainly not comparing, and He loves to hear our voice! We should be examples to our children and others around us as they hear us pray.

Every year, as part of one of my lessons, I ask the question, "Does God always answer our prayers?" And every year, I most often get the response of, "No, not always." What I quickly realized was that in their childlike way, if they do not get what they have asked for, they think God has not answered their prayers. Then I have the chance to explain to them that God does answer all of our prayers but in different ways. He does not always answer them in the way we want with an answer of "yes." Many times it is an answer of "not right now," or sometimes it is an answer of "no." We must acknowledge, they are all answers.

I think God loves to hear the prayers of children because of their childlike faith. They ask…believing! We, too, should ask in the same way.

Dear Heavenly Father, Thank You for the gift of being able to come to You and pray whenever and wherever we want. Thank You for never being too busy to hear us. Thank You for the blessing of Your children, and I pray they would hear us as examples to them of how to pray and as encouragers in their own prayers. Help us remember that You are always answering us, even in the silent times, and to remember that You are giving us what we need, not necessarily what we want. We love You, Father! In Jesus' name, Amen.

~ Julie Ray, first grade teacher

Longing

Whom have I in heaven but you?
And there is nothing on earth that I desire besides you.

Psalm 73:25, ESV

~

"It was when I was happiest that I longed most...the sweetest thing in all my life has been the longing...to find the place where all the beauty came from."[1]

Sitting on a sandy beach at sunset gazing over the sea and longing to embark upon a journey to discover what lies beyond.

Standing on the tarmac of an airport watching jets soar up into the sky and yearning to fly to adventurous places far away.

Waiting impatiently and eagerly the arrival of Christmas morning, realizing that the experience of anticipation is often more enjoyable than the real thing.

> **Intense desires and deep longings can be understood only in the light of the gospel.**

Hiking up a mountain that is so majestic and unreachable, yet craving to conquer its pinnacle. These are the idea of a deep want for something we cannot yet describe, yet is hinted at through all our greatest loves and desires, an inconsolable longing in the human heart "for which we know not what."

This longing, this yearning, this deep desiring is imprinted upon each one of us by our Creator, for "God has set eternity in the human heart, yet no one can fathom what God has done from beginning to end" (Eccl. 3:11). Life is a journey of wandering towards the true source of joy – towards one's real "home," and these intense desires and deep longings can be understood only in the light of the gospel and ultimately fulfilled through the mercy, grace, and love of Jesus Christ. It is what we were made for as humans: to long for God and ultimately to be united with Him. "For Thou [God] has made us for Thyself and our hearts are restless until they rest in Thee."[2]

O Lord, You created me with deep longings and desires; You made me to long for You. Keep me from chasing one pursuit after another attempting to find satisfaction in broken cisterns that can never satisfy. Bring me home each time to You and fill me with the living water that will ever quench the thirst of my soul.

~ A 38-year educator

Walking Faithfully

But Noah found favor in the eyes of the LORD. . . .Noah was a righteous man,
blameless among the people of his time, and he walked faithfully with God.

Genesis 6:8-9, NIV

~

Upon reading the story of the flood, it is easy to focus on the basics: Noah as the only righteous man at that time in history, the explicit instructions for the ark, the do-over God generously gave the human race, or the symbolism of the rainbow. Growing up in the church, I had many opportunities to hear the story and complete the fun leaflet activities. I remember one teacher who tried to change it up for us in sixth grade and made us act out the account by turning the table and chairs into the ark.

Model what an intimate relationship with the Lord looks like.

It was not until I was an adult who had stopped attending church that another aspect of the story popped out—Noah's faithfulness. I had officially hit the lowest point of my life when a friend suggested that perhaps I did not know the Lord at all; for certainly, someone who walked with the Lord would not be living the lifestyle I had chosen. I was so offended that I shut her out for a while, but her words echoed within me and kept me awake many nights.

She was right. I was well-versed on the stories in the Bible, but I did not know Him and most certainly did not walk with Him. I will be forever grateful for her confronting me to bring about a very convicting realization.

As parents, we are dedicated to doing the best job we can for our children. Yes, it is so important to take our children to church and Sunday school and to have them involved in service and the various programs our church offers. However, just taking them there and teaching them the stories and the verses is not enough.

We must model for our children what an intimate relationship with the Lord looks like. Let them see you reading His Word and applying it! They should be witnesses to us walking faithfully with God. Then, when the flood of temptation rises, they know that their Heavenly Father graciously gives them an ark to board.

continued

Lord Jesus, I come before You, humbled that You want to walk with me. I thank You for the relationship we have. I ask You to help me show my family what walking with You looks like, and I pray that they will want to walk with You—to know You intimately—and that their relationship with You will carry them through the challenges life has to offer. I love you, Lord. Amen.

~ Alethea Beasley, educator

Be Steadfast

Therefore, my dear brothers and sisters, stand firm. Let nothing move you. Always give yourselves fully to the work of the lord, because you know that your labor in the Lord is not in vain.

I Corinthians 15:58, NIV

~

As a Christian teacher in a Christian school, I find this verse most comforting. I hope Christian parents raising their children find comfort in this verse as well. I think the key for us all to remember is that our "…labor is not in vain in the Lord." A Christian teacher or parent should be doing everything "in the Lord." If we are not in fellowship with God, it's going to be difficult to be laboring in the Lord.

> We are to be steadfast, standing firm.

My hope is that teachers and parents realize that we are all on the same team, and our opponent is the devil. When we work together, we win together. I also believe that if we lose, it is because we did not work together. Life is busy. But let us not forget what our overall goals are. I think a good place to start is for all of us to realize that we are to be steadfast, standing firm, and laboring in the Lord every day.

Dear Lord, Help us educate Your children at school and at home exactly the way You want them educated. Help us as teachers and parents prepare them for the life You will call them to live. Give us the strength and courage to be steadfast in this most high calling. Let this all be done for Your honor and glory. Amen.

~ Matt Shelton, secondary mathematics teacher

The Call

A third time the LORD called, "Samuel!" And Samuel got up and went to Eli and said, "Here I am; you called me." Then Eli realized that the LORD was calling the boy. So Eli told Samuel, "Go and lie down, and if he calls you, say, 'Speak, LORD, for your servant is listening.'" So Samuel went and lay down in his place. The LORD came and stood there, calling as at the other times, "Samuel! Samuel!" Then Samuel said, "Speak, for your servant is listening."

I Samuel 3:8-10, NIV

~

Samuel was about twelve years old when the Lord called him. However, because Samuel could not discern the voice of the Lord, it was Eli's responsibility to direct him, not just in whom to answer but in how to answer.

We all have been faced with a "calling" situation where we needed to make a decision and dealt with the internal conflict that went along with distinguishing whether we were simply listening to our earthly desires or truly receiving direction from the Holy Spirit. Honestly, there have been times in my life when the Lord had to call me at least three times, like he did Samuel, before I finally realized it was Him because initially, I tried to logically process the situation like Samuel. Our children will face similar experiences; and like Samuel, they can be grade school age when they feel an anointing on their lives.

They feel conviction that their calling is from the Holy Spirit.

As parents, we can guide our children through these initial experiences so they are equipped to make important decisions later in life. Urging them to be regularly in the Word and to go to Him in prayer opens up their communication with Him. Then, when they feel their calling, we can show them how to respectfully ask for wisdom and discernment through their seeking process. We can model for them the practice of being in the midst of fellow believers who offer godly counsel and confirmation. When they feel conviction that their calling is from the Holy Spirit, we can encourage them to trust in the grace of our Savior and answer like the prophet Isaiah, "Here am I, send me" (Isaiah 6:9, NIV).

Lord, You know the plans You have for us, to prosper us and not harm us (Jer. 29:11). I pray for the child You so graciously gave me, and I ask that You help me train him in the way he should go. I pray that he will be able to hear the voice of the Holy Spirit in his life and answer Your special calling. I praise You for Your omniscience, grace, and unconditional love. Amen.

~ Teacher

Faithful Perseverance

*Since then we have a great high priest who has passed through the heavens,
Jesus, the Son of God, let us hold fast our confession.*

Hebrews 4:14, ESV

~

Even in our faith, sometimes life is like the roller coaster you never wanted to board but cannot get off until it has finished its full and frightening course.

Be encouraged! When circumstances cause you to feel disoriented, there is an ever-present anchor. Do not let exhaustion or fear keep you from clinging tightly to the peace that passes all understanding.

Be reminded! Peace is not a concept as the world thinks of it. Peace is a person. Jesus Christ became our Peace when he laid down his life and became our High Priest. Let your Peace make you a blessing to others all the way through any unwanted circumstances!

My "prayer" is a poem I wrote based on chapters 2-5 of Hebrews. May you be blessed with His peace in the midst of trials:

White Knuckles

The Word is the builder of all that is made,
Wants trust without doubting; flesh seen soon will fade.
May God's gracious Spirit have reign to pursue me,
Fair Lord, blind my eyes to those things that undo me.

Draw close! Draw close! Neglect leads to drifting.
Restrain, Holy Ghost! Keep my heart safe from sifting.
No longer a slave to the world, flesh, and fear,
Unchained by Another; a Brother so dear!

My Savior, my Jesus, wore flesh just like me,
Though tempted and taunted, the Lamb died sin free!
Partake, ransomed self, of that high heavenly calling,
My Priest interceded; I'm freed from free falling!

Hold fast and hold firm while today is still here!
White knuckles, hang tight! Don't let go! Persevere!
Embrace the long race, finish strong, finish best,
In my Stronghold, my Sabbath, my Sweet Place of Rest.

~ Greg Finch, 20-year teacher and parent

Daily Walk

And you shall carefully teach them [God's laws] to your sons, and shall talk of them when you sit in your house and when you walk by the way, and when you lie down, and when you rise up.

Deuteronomy 6:7, NASB

~

Before our children were born, my husband and I had decided that every evening before putting them to bed, we would read the Bible and pray with them. True to that decision we made, we began even before they could understand what was going on to do our daily routine and establish a habit of spending time with God. As our children got a little older, they began to look forward to these times with God and learning about Him. We feel that our children have been blessed by this special activity and would recommend it to every parent.

> In everything we do every day instill God's word.

Now our children are grown and have children of their own. As they look back to their childhood years, they fondly remember these times as a family; but they say that is not where they really learned to follow God. Instead, they feel they really learned about God and what He is like as we talked about God in daily conversation and made daily situations center around God and His will. They learned about God by the way we reacted and dealt with life's situations.

According to Deuteronomy 6:7, we are to teach our children daily in everything we do. We teach patience by being patient, love by showing love, how to have peace by having peace, obedience to God by being obedient, etc. While having a daily special time we spend with God and our children is certainly a starting point, it is only a beginning of what Scripture commands about how we are to continually in everything we do every day instill God's Word and principles in their hearts.

Dear Father, Help me be always aware of what I might teach my children in everyday life. I pray I will be able to show forth Christ in every situation I must face so my children might learn how to live godly. I will also do my best to spend time every day in Your Word with my children. Thank You, Father, Amen.

~ Veteran teacher

Pray Big

*I tell you the truth, if anyone says to this mountain, 'Go, throw yourself into the sea,'
and does not doubt in his heart but believes that what he says will happen,
it will be done for him. Therefore I tell you, whatever you ask for in prayer,
believe that you have received it, and it will be yours.*

Mark 11:23–24, NIV

~

When: First century BC
Where: Israel
Who: Honi, the circle maker
What: A big prayer

The story of Honi is found in the Talmud, and the lesson is good.

The land had gone without rain for a year and everyone had given up on God, except Honi. As thousands of Israelites watched, he prayed a big prayer and believed God, and God heard him and responded with the soaking rain they had needed for months. If this actually happened, it was a prayer that changed the course of Israel's history. All because one man refused to give up on God and prayed a big prayer. Of course, the Bible is full of stories of ordinary people who prayed big prayers that were answered by God such as Elijah's prayer for resurrection of the widow's son (1 Kings 17).

In his book, *The Circle Maker*, Mark Batterson states, "God isn't offended by your biggest dreams or boldest prayers. He is offended by anything less. If your prayers aren't impossible to you, they are insulting to God."[3] There have been times in my life when I got stuck in the rut of just praying for the bare minimum. You know, asking God for my daily needs of food, home, and for protection and good health for my loved ones. While those are good to pray for and we should be praying those prayers, God wants and expects so much more. He wants to bless us with an abundant life (John 10:10, NKJV).

*Father God, "Who is able to do immeasurably more than all we ask or imagine,"
(Ephesians 3:20) teach us to pray big prayers, expecting You to answer. Amen.*

~ Mrs. Schmidt, junior high advisor

Relationship vs. Religion

Not everyone who says to me, 'Lord, Lord,' will enter the kingdom of heaven, but only he who does the will of my Father who is in heaven. Many will say to me on that day, 'Lord, Lord, did we not prophesy in your name, and in your name drive out demons and perform many miracles?' Then I will tell them plainly, 'I never knew you. Away from me, you evildoers!

Matthew 7:21-23, NIV

~

In this Scripture Christ is calling us into a relationship with Him. He compares us to a tree bearing good or bad fruit (the fruit of our spirit). To be a tree which bears good fruit, we must be a strongly rooted tree. If we are a tree bearing bad fruit, our root system is obviously not stable. To strengthen our root system and bear good fruit, we must be in a connected, growing relationship with our Lord and Savior. Christ goes on to say in this passage that those trees bearing bad fruit must be cut down and thrown into the fire. The word picture that we see unfold has to do with a relationship vs. religious acts.

Webster's definition of:
Relationship ~ link or connection; being related; maintaining good connections with a member of family
Religion ~ belief in gods or in one God; system of worship[4]

We [the tree] can look like a Christian, act like a Christian, worship every Sunday, read Scripture, serve on ministry teams, join small groups, wear Christian t-shirts, and listen to Christian music…and still not have a relationship with Christ. Religion will not save us, only Jesus can. We can have a plethora of religion and never experience the life-giving and liberating power of the Holy Spirit in our day-to-day life, if we have not come to surrender our hearts to Christ and knowing Him. True life (healthy tree life) begins by inviting Christ into your heart and staying rooted in Him. Indeed, we are identified by fruit both now and in eternity. Grow strong and deep in His soil!

> **Religion will not save us, only Jesus can.**

Heavenly Father, Someday I want to stand before You and hear 'Well done good and faithful servant.' Grow me closer to You, Lord, no matter what it takes. I do not want to simply look and act the part; I want to be one with You. I want to be a healthy tree growing healthy fruit to further Your Kingdom. Show me, Lord, what You would have me do, where You would have me go, what You would have me say to help plant and/or multiply other healthy trees. Amen.

~ Sarah Hardinger, teacher

True Children

What's more, the Scriptures looked forward to this time when God would accept the Gentiles, too, on the basis of their faith. God promised this good news to Abraham long ago when he said, "All nations will be blessed through you." And so it is: All who put their faith in Christ share the same blessing Abraham received because of his faith… And now that you belong to Christ, you are the true children of Abraham. You are his heirs, and now all the promises God gave to him belong to you.

Galatians 3:8-9; 29, NLT

~

Jesus did not promise we would not have problems.

Now all the promises God gave to him belong to you! This is such good news; no wonder Jesus himself described His ministry as "good news" When introducing Himself in the synagogue, He said, quoting Isaiah 61:1-2, "The spirit of the Lord is upon me, for He has appointed me to preach Good News to the poor…" There are many other places, too, that He describes His message as Good News. In the fact, the word Gospel means "good news!"

Over and over Jesus points back to the blessing of Abraham and the promised inheritance of the descendants of Abraham. Then we learn in Galatians, among other places, that those descendants…they are us! Those promised blessing are for every single person that puts faith in Jesus. Praise the Lord!

In the past several years I have been so very blessed to learn more and more about this blessing of Abraham, but I have noticed sometimes that even Christians have a hard time believing in the promises. Hosea warns that "My people are destroyed for lack of knowledge…" (Hosea 4:6, ESV). I challenge you to study out the Scriptures and the blessing that Jesus so joyfully talked about everywhere He went. You will find that studying Deuteronomy 28 is a great place to start.

Once we truly get a hold of who we really are in Christ, Satan cannot stop us. Sickness…worry about our kids…finances…pressure…none of these can match the provision of the blessing of Abraham. Jesus did not promise we would not have problems, but He did promise we are overcomers! The blessing overcomes just like He did when He overcame the world! Hallelujah!

Heavenly Father, Thank You for sending Your son to die for me so that I may receive the inheritance of Abraham. I acknowledge with my faith that the very reason Jesus was sacrificed was to take away my sin and bring me into unity with You and everything You are and everything You have. Teach me, Lord, more about who You are, what You have promised and how to live with respect to those promises. Help me NOT to pattern my life on what other people say, but on what You say. Amen.

~ An educator

Faithful Prayer

I exhort therefore, that, first of all, supplications, prayers, intercessions,
and giving of thanks, be made for all men.

I Timothy 2:1, KJV

~

We should pray faithfully every day. Let us examine the four things the Bible outlines about prayer.

Supplication ~ *Prayer for our needs.*
Rejoice in the Lord always: and again I say, Rejoice. Let your moderation be known unto all men. The Lord is at hand. Be careful for nothing; but in everything by prayer and supplication with thanksgiving let your requests be made known unto God. (Philippians 4:4-7, KJV)

Prayers ~ *Psalms.*
For thou, O Lord of hosts, God of Israel, hast revealed to thy servant, saying, I will build thee a house: therefore hath thy servant found in his heart to pray this prayer unto thee. (II Samuel 7:27, KJV)

Intercessions ~ *Prayer for the needs of others.*
Ye also helping together by prayer for us, that for the gift bestowed upon us by the means of many persons thanks may be given by many on our behalf. (II Corinthians 1:11, KJV)

Giving thanks to God ~ *For what He has done for us.*
And Hannah prayed, and said, My heart rejoiceth in the Lord, mine horn is exalted in the Lord: my mouth is enlarged over mine enemies; because I rejoice in thy salvation…. (I Samuel 2:1-10, KJV)

Father in Heaven, Let Your words; not man's words, permeate our hearts and guide our actions all of our days. Let our faithful prayers be pleasing to You and thank You for listening. Amen.

~ Matt Shelton, secondary mathematics teacher

Teachable Moments

Fix these words of mine in your hearts and minds; tie them as symbols on your hands and bind them on your foreheads. Teach them to your children, talking about them when you sit at home and when you walk along the road, when you lie down and when you get up.

Deuteronomy 11:18-19, NIV

~

This side of heaven we may never know who we have touched for eternity. I tell my students that more than anything, I want to spend eternity with each and every one of them. I jokingly promise them that I will not give them any homework in heaven. In reality, I love those times when God shows up and nudges me to take time to spotlight Him. It is my prayer that I am able to seize those moments throughout my school day to provide nuggets of Who God is to each of my students.

Find teachable moments in the daily routine.

In the course of a school year, things get misplaced. I will often suggest that a student pray for God to help in the recovery. I delight when a student prays for an important item, such as a completed assignment, to be found. God so often comes through right in that moment. I will smile and simply respond, "See how God takes care of you!" What a simple, yet powerful testimony to our God. To give God the glory is so much more beautiful than chalking it up to luck. I believe through this gentle nudging and teaching of how God works, we can and will impact others to spend eternity in the presence of our Heavenly Father. I believe that there is great power in taking every opportunity to spotlight God in all aspects of our lives. Sometimes, He acts in big ways, but often it is when we find teachable moments in the daily routine of life that His power and majesty can be displayed.

In the small things, in the life-changing things, in all things, Father, work in our hearts to trust You. May we have the faith to see You in all circumstances of our lives. May we give You all the praise and glory in our lives. Help us to impact others in profound ways that they may spend eternity with You. Amen.

~ Michelle Bacon, fifth-grade teacher

Personal Doubt

…you must believe and not doubt, because the one who doubts is like a wave of the sea, blown and tossed by the wind. That person should not expect to receive anything from the Lord. Such a person is double-minded and unstable in all they do.

James 1:6-8, NIV

~

Have you ever doubted yourself? I know I have! Doubt is a tool that Satan likes to use against us! Doubt usually creeps in when we are not trusting in God and His perfect plans for us. Doubt crawls in like a slimy worm when we are not confident in our Lord, making us afraid of what could happen in the future. When you feel that wiggling worm of fear, ask yourself, "Am I really trusting in You right now, Lord?" Truly, Satan knows how to get in our mind and play those recorded tapes of "You can't do it" over and over.

We can do anything and everything with the help of Christ Jesus our Lord! Do not believe that you cannot do something because of doubt! Satan is using this against you to break you down. Satan can and will play the tapes of doubt in your head because he is looking to devour you and your walk with Christ.

Do not let doubt be your Mount Everest.

The good news is that there is nothing impossible with God. Our weaknesses are made strong in Him, and we can be confident that our submitted life is under His full control.

Do not let doubt be your Mount Everest. You can do it through your amazing Lord Who will take care of you and open doors for you if you do away with doubt.

You can do all things when you are strong in the Lord and in His mighty power (Philippians 4:13, NIV).

Dear Lord, Help me to be confident in You instead of doubting that we are able to do something. With You, nothing is impossible! It is so encouraging to know that You are our mighty power. Work in me and restore my spirits when I am weak and doubting. I love You.

~ Mrs. Bethany L., sixth-grade teacher

Guarding Generations

After that whole generation had been gathered to their ancestors, another generation grew up who knew neither the Lord nor what he had done for Israel. Then the Israelites did evil in the eyes of the Lord and served the Baals. They forsook the Lord, the God of their ancestors, who had brought them out of Egypt. They followed and worshiped various gods of the peoples around them.

Judges 2:10-12, NIV

~

Why did a whole generation turn away from the Lord to serve the gods of their time? The issue was disobedience by their parents. The Israelites did not obey God and drive out the inhabitants as they conquered the land; instead, the Israelites allowed the inhabitants to live among them. Sometimes we look at passages of Scripture and criticize the people we read about, but these passages reflect our own tendencies and their eventual consequences.

Demonstrate a life of obedience. God has called us to drive everything out of our lives and make Him first; but just like the children of Israel, we allow certain things to rule in our lives that eventually become a stumbling block to us as parents and an idol for our children. I have been a club soccer coach for over fourteen years; and if you are involved with any kind of club sport, you know there are some challenges to living your life for Christ so that sport does not become an idol. When I began coaching, I made a commitment that I would not compromise Sunday worship services for a season game; and after all of these years, there have been only a handful of times where this was not the case. My wife and I did not want to compromise on the important spiritual discipline of worshiping God with His people because the spiritual development of our family was more important than the demands and lifestyle of a sport. Each family will approach decisions differently, but obedience to God's commands will guard our families from idols inhabiting our homes.

Examine your life right now. What do you need to drive out of your life so your family can follow God wholeheartedly? The call to obedience is more rewarding than the consequences of disobedience. We cannot compromise the spiritual future of our children. One of the greatest gifts you can give to your family kids is to demonstrate a life of obedience in your walk with Christ by keeping idols out of your home.

Lord, My desire is to see my kids following You. Please help me expose those areas of my life that I have not completely surrendered to You. Give me the courage and strength to identify anything that is an obstacle for me and a future idol for my kids. Teach me what it means to live a life of obedience.

~ Emir A. Ruiz-Esparza, secondary principal

Plainly See

They replied, "We can plainly see that the Lord is with you…" [Abimelech speaking to Jacob after observing his great wealth from the blessing of the Lord.]

Genesis 26:28, RSV

~

Nobody has to tell us that there are evil people in the world. Many of the ungodly have figured out a way to create temporary wealth for themselves. Sadly, some Christians get the idea that being wealthy is evil. I have encountered this attitude while teaching a personal finance class. Some students really have a hard time accepting that it is ok to "build wealth and give," as Dave Ramsey puts it.[5]

But God has a plan to bless the righteous. He began the plan back in Genesis 12 when He said to Abraham that he would bless him and make him famous in order to be a blessing to others.

I have taught the students to never forget the plan in this entire blessing is to be able to be a blessing to others. Think about it: no missionary can travel without the faithful giving of believers. No VBS could happen without all those donated supplies! There is absolutely nothing wrong with being blessed. God does have some advice for His people who are 'rich in this world':

> **There is absolutely nothing wrong with being blessed.**

I Timothy 6:17-19: Tell those who are rich in this world not to be proud and not to trust in their money which will soon be gone. But their trust should be in the living God, who richly gives us all we need for our enjoyment. Tell them to use their money to do good. They should be rich in good works and should give generously to those in need, always being ready to share with others whatever God has given them. By doing this they will be storing up their treasure as a good foundation for the future so that they may take hold of real life. (emphasis mine)

This world contains those who are perishing for lack of knowledge. This world needs to plainly see that God blesses and increases His people!

Dear Father, Help me to remember to never be ashamed of the blessings You have given us. Please help me to remember we are to be a source and a symbol of Your BLESSING to many nations! Help me to always be faithful in my finances and be obedient to Your word that says be ready to share with others whatever You have given me. Amen.

~ Mrs. Seale, business

Joyful Parenting

Thou wilt shew me the path of life:
in thy presence is fullness of joy;
at thy right hand there are
pleasures for evermore.
Psalms 16:11, KJV

Life Everywhere!

I have come that they may have life, and that they may have it more abundantly.

John 10:10, NKJV

~

> **But Christ came to bring Life—Life with a capital L.**

"A picture paints a thousand words." In Russian artist Nikolai Yaroshenko's famous painting *Life Is Everywhere*,[6] we see depicted a trainload of convicted criminals on their way to Siberian exile and imprisonment. The picture was painted under the inspiration of a story by Leo Tolstoy entitled "What do People Cherish in Life?" The artist originally planned to call his work *Where there is love, there is God*. In the forward window, the prisoners have crowded together to feed pigeons. They are colorful, smiling, and in the midst of their bleak circumstance, cherishing goodness, celebrating life. At the back of the car, there stands one lonely silhouetted figure facing away, not realizing the beauty and goodness that still exists.

Life not engaged with God and the beauty and goodness that He brings, even in the midst of a sinful, broken world, can only remain just that—lifeless. But Christ came to bring Life—Life with a capital L, enjoying the fullness of His presence in all that He has created, even in the midst of great trial, sorrow, and affliction. "And this is eternal life that they know you, the only true God, and Jesus Christ, whom you have sent" (John 17:3, NIV).

Lord, Life can be dark and bleak and broken; but in the midst of all that I must face, bring me to places of joy and beauty. Give me simple places where I can say, "That is beautiful! Lord, You are good!"

~ **Donna Eames, a 38-year educator**

Look! Look!

Shout for joy to God, all the earth!
Sing the glory of His name; make His praise glorious.

Psalm 66: 1-2, NIV

~

Oh boy, am I easily amazed, entertained and fascinated! The first butterfly of spring? I stop dead in my tracks, face glowing with surprise, and then happily blurt out, "Look! Look!" A beautiful blue sky, complimented with a smattering of big, puffy clouds, and the sunlight shining *just right* that makes everything look so alive? "Look! Look!" I just cannot help it!

God has given us so much to see, experience and enjoy! I feel the joy bursting from the psalmist as he continues in chapter 66, verses 3-5, *"Say to God, 'Your works are amazing! Because your power is great, your enemies fall before you. All the earth worships you and sings praises to you. They sing praises to your name. Come and see what God has done, the amazing things he has done for people."* As we are out and about, I am constantly pointing out what God has done.

My family just smiles and smiles (and sometimes laughs!) as I eagerly tell them to "Look! Look! Look what God has done!" When we are passionate about these seemingly "little things" that God has done, our family will start to notice them too. While we all have different personality types and may not squeal with delight (me!) upon encountering a little piece of God's goodness, the heart will respond.

So much to see, experience and enjoy!

Dear Jesus, Thank You for all the glorious things You have done! Thank You for all the glorious things we can experience! Thank You for the simple things that make our hearts swell with joy as we call out, "Look! Look!" In Jesus' Name, Amen.

~ Mrs. @, who sings praises daily!

Simply Smile

May the God of hope fill you with all joy and peace in believing, so that by the power of the Holy Spirit you may abound in hope.

Romans 15:13, NASB

~

When I was young, my mom would sometimes wake me up singing "Rise and shine and give God the glory, glory." After hearing that, I would feel like it was wrong to complain about having to get up to go to school. Now that I do not live at home anymore, I sometimes have to pep talk myself to put a smile on my face about getting up early and going to work. You do not really have to go to school or work with a smile on your face, but I realized one thing early in my teaching career: A smile is contagious. I know you have probably heard it a lot, but it is so true. If I walk into the gym with a smile on my face, the kids share the emotion with me. I also realized that it is part of my job to put that smile on their faces. My goal each day is to end class in such a way that they will leave with a smile; and hopefully, it will help their attitude for the rest of the day.

A smile is contagious.

What kind of attitude are we showing our children in the morning right when they wake up? On the way to school? When we drop them off? We must always remember the impact our attitude has on theirs; and if we want Christ to shine through them, it must first shine through us.

Dear Lord, Be with me today as I go through my day, and help me keep a smile on my face and joy in my heart. Let my kids see the joy that You bring me every day in my expression and speech. Thank You for giving me so many reasons to be joyful.

~ Coach "Ammo" Siemsen, PE teacher & soccer coach

Consider Joy

Consider it pure joy, my brothers, whenever you face trials of many kinds, because you know that the testing of your faith develops perseverance.

James 1:2-3, NIV

~

Consider it joy when you face a trial? This does not sound quite right by the standards of the world today. In today's world, most people are expecting things to go their way, or life seems unfair. We have all probably been in places be fore where life doesn't seem to be going the way it looked in our childhood dreams or even what we had planned in our young adult lives. I admit that I, too, have been placed on a path that had never appeared in the "map" I had planned for my future.

He has chosen me for certain trials for a specific reason.

That's when I began to realize the problem. It was my map, not His. Oh, it is easy to resist following His map, if we choose; but it is when we finally realize He had our best interest at heart when He created it, that we learn to trust Him and look for joy along the ride.

When we face trials, we will be led in one of two directions. We will move closer to God, or we will move farther away from Him. I would have never dreamed that I could consider the trials I have faced to be joyful experiences. I would have never dreamed the hard things I have gone through would have brought me closer to Him, but by His grace, they have. It is not easy to be happy through them, but happiness is very different from joyfulness. Joy comes from within our heart, and it is a choice we have to make.

I have come to realize that He has chosen me for certain trials for a specific reason. I am trying to learn not to compare my life with someone else's. Our paths are unique to us, and for that, we should be grateful.

Dear Heavenly Father, I thank You for the path You have orchestrated for my life. Forgive me for the times I've tried to alter Your path and make it my own. Though the trials have been tough, I thank You for walking with me every step of the way and for the wonderful godly people You have put with me along my journey to help make the path easier. Give me Your wisdom and insight as new trials come my way and help me remember to give thanks for the peaceful times in between. May I consider it joy in all situations when You entrust me with a trial You have chosen for me, and may I grow ever closer to You in the process.

~ Julie Ray, first-grade teacher

God's Funny

...the joy of the Lord is your strength.

Nehemiah 8:10b, KJV

~

Christianity is supposed to be joyful.

One look at the creation around you, and you know God's funny. We have anteaters and hippopotami. We have fluffy fungus, and we eat it. Baby everythings are awesome! Do not forget the funny Bible stories: Sarah pregnant in her 90s, Namaan washing leprosy in the disgusting river, and Balaam's donkey!

Christianity is supposed to be joyful—and so is parenting. In a fallen world where Satan is continually at work to take us out of the picture, it is critical that we remember that from joy is the strength to enable his defeat! We must work diligently to create settings where those around us can feel that joy.

Parents can alleviate many poor attitudes in their children if they enable a setting that produces laughter in the midst of work. For example, those Saturday morning chores can get to all of us. Occasionally, I will write our chores on paper and throw them folded individually into a bowl. You "git what you git, and you don't throw a fit." is the motto. Favorites in this for my children are my special chores: do a Woobie Dance (No such thing, I wanted to see what they made up), stand on the couch and yell, "My mom is gorgeous!" five times, etc. It was also interesting to see which kid pulled out "clean the fridge." I had to flex on the perfection of accomplishment—so worth it to laugh throughout our work time.

Dear parent, you set the tone. Always. Choose joy as the soil in which you grow your kids.

Lord, I love how You are all-powerful and mighty, but still take time to ensure those You love can laugh. I really love how laughing even helps me burn calories! HA! That is so awesome. God, let me be the person others want to see coming their way. Let my words bring smiles, and my presence reflect the God Who is mighty and still prioritizes joy. Love ya!

~ A teacher seriously in love with Jesus

Nice Try

I prayed to the Lord, and he answered me. He freed me from all my fears. Those who look to him for help will be radiant with joy; no shadow of shame will darken their faces.

Psalm 34:4-5, NLT

~

The kids and I were playing in the woods where there was a small creek running through a wooded area. Here I noticed a huge tree that had fallen, creating a perfect log bridge. I remembered climbing trees and playing in creeks as a child growing up in the country, so my immediate instinct was to walk across the log to the other side.

My kids saw me do it and wanted to try, too. My son slowly crept across with my verbal guidance reminding him to walk really slowly and watch where he was stepping. He did it! Then my daughter Emma wanted to attempt what we had both done. She tentatively said, "I can try." She went about five feet

Willingness to persevere will result in exultation!

across and stopped because she was too scared to continue. I went up on the log and helped her down. She tried one more time a little later, and the same thing happened. After seeing her brother go back and forth several times, she wanted to give it a third shot. She repeated the phrase, "I can try." I said, "Yes, you can try. That's all we can do is just keep trying." She moved incredibly slowly, pausing after a few steps and looking to me for encouragement. She ended up successfully going across the fallen tree several times before we left, and you could not imagine her radiant joy when she completed her task each time!

Don't we have a fear of failure a lot of times? We may even begin a task or feel that God gives us a certain goal, but we hesitate to move forward to completion for fear that we cannot do it. God showed me through my daughter that a willingness to persevere will result in exultation! He will even coach us! Just as she needed my constant encouragement, Christ will be there for us as we go along our task. We teach our children to keep practicing and try again at things, but we sometimes stop making an effort as adults.

What would you do if you were not afraid to fail? We can walk in fullness of joy by confessing those fears and asking Him to help us be the overcomers He has called us to be.

God, Help me listen to what You tell me to do and take every step in faith as I go. Just as my child slowly walked across the fallen tree when she was scared, help me act in the midst of my fears, allowing Your voice to be my guide into joy. Amen.

~ Mrs. Schueller, fourth-grade teacher

Big Rocks

For the kingdom of God is not a matter of what we eat or drink,
but of living a life of goodness and peace and joy in the Holy Spirit.

Romans 14:17, NLT

~

The spiritual rocks on God's list: a life of righteousness and peace and joy.

Decades ago I attended a Franklin Covey workshop on time management. Actually, I think his system was more about life management. One illustration stuck with me. The presenter filled a large jar with tiny pebbles then tried to add three larger rocks. He couldn't. Then he dumped out the jar and put the three larger rocks in first. When he poured the same stack of tiny pebbles into the jar, they all fit! The point he made was simple, but like lots of simple things, it was profound. Each day, he advised, select the three biggest rocks on your list, the ones that MUST GET DONE!! My tendency is to cross off all the little things first, but that results in the "it's midnight, and I have not started the project I am supposed to give to my boss tomorrow" panic. The results are much better when I start my day tackling my "three big rocks." I cannot say all my pebbles fit into the day, but I do not have as many midnight panics. So, what are the spiritual three big rocks on God's list? It is living a life of righteousness and peace and joy in the Holy Spirit and showing others how to do the same.

Please help us, Lord. Too many of our days resemble the to-do list that must have been on Martha's mind when Jesus showed up at her house for dinner! Help us filter our list through Your list. Keep us plugged into the Holy Spirit and Your resurrection power so that Your kingdom of righteousness, peace, and joy reigns today.

~ Mrs. Terry, social studies

Expecting Joy

But the angel said to them, "Do not be afraid; for behold, I bring you
good news of great joy which will be for all the people."

Luke 2:10, NASB

~

Joy is an interesting word that can be defined in many ways. For a Christian, joy should be defined by its source: Jesus.

Life, in general, throws all kinds of people and situations into our daily walks that might remove that joy. For instance, my wife is working full time and finishing a master's degree. The stress that this can cause is almost incalculable, but to those who are faithful and persevere despite trials--God brings the blessings! These blessings bring great joy.

In our stressful and hectic situation, the Lord brought my wife and I great joy through expecting a child. When she revealed to me that I was a dad, I wept because of all the happiness that filled my heart. Becoming a father (Baby due in a few short months) has already changed my life. I look at the world around me totally differently. I find hope in the fact that my child will grow up knowing Christ and will spread the joy Christ brings to all.

> Joy should be defined by its source: Jesus.

As Christians we can confidently expect our heavenly Father to be the source of never-ending joy. His abundant love and blessings need only to be embraced.

Lord, You know when we are suffering and need more of You. Lord, please let us seek You in the those times that we might find joy in You alone. None could ask for a greater gift than to forever live with the abundant source of joy that is Jesus Christ. And Lord, in this moment, I give You great praise for the sweet joy that is our children.

~ Austin Strange, future daddy and business teacher

Parenting Parables

A farmer went out to sow his seed. As he was scattering the seed, some fell along the path; it was trampled on, and the birds ate it up. Some fell on rocky ground, and when it came up, the plants withered because they had no moisture. Other seed fell among thorns, which grew up with it and choked the plants. Still other seed fell on good soil. It came up and yielded a crop, a hundred times more than was sown. When he said this, he called out, "Whoever has ears to hear, let them hear."

Luke 8:5-10, NIV

~

Do not become discouraged in joyfully throwing God's Word.

A family translation might go like this:

A parent went out to raise a family. In expectant joy, God's words were spread for the children to hear. In shattered hope, it was recognized some words fell on children who were too busy to hear and obey. One child laughed at the foolishness of his parents. Some children heard, but did not apply the words to their lives. Thankfully, some words fell on children that were willing to hear and obey.

We are ecstatic for those children who understand the sowing the first time. What to do with the others? Remember, farmers sow over and over and over again. Each time the seeds go out, the hope is rejoicing over the harvest.

As parents and teachers, our job is to share God's Word. Sometimes our children "get it," and other times it seems to fall on deaf ears. Though we often wonder, "Why did not they understand? Did I sow my seeds poorly?" The resounding answer is, "No!" We just need to do our job until the Lord returns. It is up to God to inspire the child to use or apply what we have said.

Do not become discouraged in joyfully throwing God's Word to your children. Discuss Bible stories and how to apply their truth to our lives. Faithfully fill their heads with God's words. Give your child a buffet table from which to choose. Someday, they will eat.

Lord, Help me to remember to share Your love and kindnesses with my children. I want my child to have Your words in their hearts. Open opportunities today to share with my child.

~ Mary Musil, second grade

Pursue Passion

Whatever you do, work at it with all your heart,
as working for the Lord, not for human masters.

Colossians 3:23, NIV

~

Always pursue your true passions. One of the scariest things I have ever done was to trade my security, take the leap of faith, and transition later in life to follow my passion. Though I was moderately happy in an established career path, I knew God was calling me to trust enough to let go of the familiar. It definitely turned into one of the best decisions of my life. My decision was initiated through reflection.

I began considering the topics that had consistently encouraged joy within my spirit. I had always loved art, even when thinking I was not good enough to pursue it at a professional level. I loved the creative process, attention to detail, and collaboration as a team required in producing something from nothing. I also loved seeing the fire light within those working alongside me. My passion for people and for art translated into becoming an art teacher. Every day is filled with the joy of knowing that I am fulfilling my creator's purpose for me.

Every day is filled with the joy of knowing that I am fulfilling my Creator's purpose.

Pursuing the passions He placed within me also encouraged deeper experiences in my walk with the Lord. I have had to walk in faith and open my eyes to see the many blessings that He provides along the way. I have learned submitted obedience to His call brings joy and passion beyond measure.

The passions and talents placed within our hearts should help guide our life's direction. Satisfaction comes from using our specific abilities and interests. When we are fulfilling our designed destiny, we can have an incomparable sense of wholeness and joy.

Lord, Thank You for putting unique passions in each of us. Help me to see and appreciate the passions in my child, so that I may encourage exploration and growth in these areas. Help us see the possibilities, have faith to seek Your will, and trust in Your provision. God, I want to model letting go of everything that keeps me from following Your perfect will for my life.

~ Jana Jurkovich, secondary art

Joyful Settings

…Strength and joy are in his dwelling place.

I Chronicles 16:27, NIV

~

Accepting Christ is life changing! My parents became Christians when I was in the third grade. Over a short amount of time, the world I had lived in became completely different. My mom, a casual smoker, immediately stopped. She said all of her desire was taken from her. Mom and dad used swear words on occasion. Words changed; the Lord gave them a heart to speak rightly. The biggest change to my third grade eyes was the new setting of our home.

Before life in Christ, we were cluttered.

Before life in Christ, we were cluttered. Not disgusting or filthy, just messy. We never had cleaning days, and my mom was fine if our toys were everywhere and the laundry piled up. Then Jesus made His presence known, and mom had a new perspective! She started our Saturday mornings with the announcements that Jesus was coming and things needed to look good! The lists came out, and we got busy. For most children, this would have been awful, but my mom always cranked her "album of the month" and go dancing around with the vacuum, cracking us up. We would sometimes stop mid-chores, grab our dolls, and boogie down to Tommy Roe's "Sweet, Little Sheila" or Kenny Rogers' "Just Dropped In."[9,10] These were not necessarily "Christian" songs, but the joy of Jesus was all over that living room.

Our home sparkled with cleaning products, and our hearts sparkled with joy and pride. Because of the presence of Jesus within my parents, my home life became more beautiful in every way: smell, sounds, and sight!

Our Savior brings joy because He cares about everything that touches our world. If we allow Him, He will take the good and make it awesome.

Father, Show me where my world can be made a more beautiful reflection of Who You are. I want people near me to see, hear, and smell the joy You bring into my life! Please enable me to be a joy giver because of Who You are in me.

~ An educator and mom of two girls and a boy!

Excited!

Jesus said, "Let the little children come to me, and do not hinder them, for the kingdom of heaven belongs to such as these.

Matthew 19:14, KJV

~

When is the last time you have been truly excited about something? For me it was the phone calls I would get from my now husband. We lived three hours apart and had to make our relationship long distance. I remember the "honeymoon" phase when we were still getting to know each other. We would talk well into the wee hours of the night! Now we are lucky if we get to even see each other at night!

Our Father longs for us to live in joy!

I thought about this idea of excitement while visiting the zoo with my kiddos the other day. While riding the sky tram, my baby girl clutched my face (ok, honestly she was slapping both cheeks) saying, "Mommy! Mommy!" She was super excited about the giraffe that was walking right under our feet. She did not just do this one time, but several as her excitement grew with each passing animal. I laugh now at the idea of "slapping" someone in the face (I would not recommend that literally) to show exultant joy at being together. I view the excitement on Hadley's sweet face when she sees the other animals as, " Look, Mom, at ALL the blessings God wants to send my way if I follow Him!"

In reflection, I must ask myself, when was the last time I got excited to talk with my Heavenly Father, to anticipate my talk with Him, to let that "phone call" to Him consume my thoughts all day? When was the last time I stayed up with Him, talking to Him in prayer into the wee hours of the night? It has been a while. And honestly, for most of us myself included, it is when we are hurting and sad, not when we just want to spend time with Him because of our excitement over having Him in our lives.

Our Father longs for us to live in joy! Let us get excited about Jesus, the One Who gave everything so that we can have eternity with Him.

I learn a lot from watching my children, as I am sure you do, too. What an amazing gift the Lord has provided to us in them, especially as they lead us into joy!

God, I pray that we would fall in joyful love with You all over again today. I pray that we would be excited to share You with others and that we would anticipate the blessings that come when we follow You. Thank You for giving the gift of salvation through Your son, Jesus. Amen.

~ Mrs. Gamber, mommy and teacher

Enjoying Jesus

*You make known to me the path of life; you will fill me with joy
in your presence, with eternal pleasures at your right hand.*

Psalm 16:11, NIV

~

"What's for dinner?" "May I go out to play?" Why do I have to clean my room?" "May I get this toy?" Why should I do my homework?" As parents, we are bombarded by questions like these and many more on a daily basis. We can take the line of questioning for a time; but when the artillery of questions flies at us without a break or pause, frustration often comes. To have an enjoyable conversation, it takes more than just questions and more than a one-sided conversation. Joy comes when we are able to talk AND listen with one another.

> **Enjoy His company and the "still small voice."**

I wonder if our Lord Jesus feels this same way when we come to Him with our laundry list of questions and requests. We do all the talking. We make sure our needs are heard, rattling on and on without stopping to truly enjoy Him. I have found myself falling into this fleshly, childish pattern on many occasions. Shortly after one of these occasions, I was asked by a friend if I was enjoying Jesus. It did not take long for me to see that I was missing out big time. Here are some thoughts that I went through in my personal evaluation.

I relish those special talk and listen conversations I have with my children, spouse, and friends. I look forward to these times with great anticipation. Why then, should it be any different with Jesus? According to John 15:4, I have the very presence of the Lord within me; I need to enjoy His company and the "still small voice" He speaks over me.

Lord, Help me relish the quiet times I have with You. Will You help me listen to Your voice? I truly want to enjoy You!

~ Mrs. Sanders, elementary vice principal

Joyful Clothing

*You turned my wailing into dancing; you removed my sackcloth
and clothed me with joy.*

Psalm 30:11, NIV

~

The day was April 1, and it ended much differently than how it started. The day began with me ripe with my first pregnancy and in the second trimester. I was on my way to pick up a friend at the airport. It ended at the hospital…dazed, confused. Mourning. Miscarriage. It was a common thing to happen, but why me, God?

> He really does transform our wailing.

There were so many reasons to be bitter, but I felt a deep tug in my heart, almost like an invitation, "Trust me. Lean into Me. I can heal your heart if you would trust Me." So just like in the Garden of Eden when God made clothing for His children, He clothed me, too. But instead of animal skins, He clothed me with joy.

The inner workings of our heart are just like garments. We wear them on our face, hold them in our eyes and carry them as we walk. I am so glad that my story of motherhood did not end in that sad hospital room. I let Him clothe me with joy; and because of this, I was able to bear the thought of having more children.

Today I have four beautiful blessings. He really does transform our wailing, remove our mourning, and clothe us with joy. Let Him transform you today.

God, Even though at times we face heartbreak and hardship, show us the way of joy. Show us that Your yoke is easy and guide us to give You our burdens. Thank You for Your joyful garments!

~ **Mrs. Nagy, band director, mother of four, clothed with joy**

Finding Joy

...Do not grieve, for the joy of the Lord is your strength.

Nehemiah 8:10b, NIV

~

Have you ever been in a place where you were faced with a painful situation and reached out to God in prayer and said, "Today is not a happy day; but I trust You, Lord, to fill me with Your joy"?

Happy is a chosen feeling; but joy is from the inside out.

As I began my teaching career, I was so excited about getting to know my students and their parents. To make a difference in the lives of these precious children and to do what I know God has called me to do has been an amazing journey.

In my first year of teaching, my exhilarating joy was mingled with a deep sorrow. My best friend, husband, and daddy to our daughter was serving our country overseas; and I was, for the first time in my adult life, faced with complete yielding to God to give me grace, one step at a time--sometimes one breath at a time. While I tried to encourage and teach my students, I also worked to encourage and comfort my own daughter, who missed her daddy. When my strength was drained at the end of the day or week, I knew where my comfort, joy, hope, and love came from—Jesus Christ, my Lord and Savior. When I paused to refocus my mind on Him, He was faithful to restore my joy.

Today, if you are challenged with a pain, a broken heart, or a situation that seems daunting or impossible, seek the face of God with your whole heart. Know that He is right there, waiting to answer your whispered prayer, your cry in pain, your need of fulfillment in any area of your life. I know firsthand that happiness is a chosen feeling; but joy is from the inside out, a gift from God.

Father God, Thank You for Your blessings and promises. Thank You for loving us when we are weak and heavy laden. I ask for Your blessing upon the beautiful families that serve You and ask You to comfort them and give them joy and peace in You. Amen.

~ Fourth-grade teacher and military wife

Greatest Joy

I have no greater joy than to hear that my children are walking in truth.

III John 1:4 ESV

~

In the book of III John, John writes to Gaius, commending him for continuing to serve the body of Christ, walking in the truth in which he had been taught. A few years ago, our school used this verse as a theme for our entire year.

As adults we are tasked with the awesome responsibility of partnering with Christ to mold our children into His image. Often the weight of the responsibility is crushing. I have heard parents and teachers alike use phrases such as "there is just so much." "I can't breathe." or "I am overwhelmed." Children are not easy; and the world often brings much against them, making the job of raising them even harder. Health issues, financial pressure, family problems—the list of hurdles is endless. We must remember that there is no promise that child raising would be without its fights.

We live in a fallen world that fights for the minds and the very lives of our children every day. There is a reason we are admonished to put on the armor of God: we are warriors in a battle. Admittedly, some days end in being bruised and feeling defeated.

But, if we *hold the line*....

John reminds us, there is no greater joy than to hear, "Your child is walking in truth!" It makes me giddy to think about it. My own children, my students— they are going to have every chance to know Jesus and be His disciple! Yeah!

> **Take courage and stand in the joy of what is coming.**

So, when the battle seems to overtake you, remember the joy on the horizon. Picture your baby standing before the Lord, hearing the words, "Well done."

Warrior, take courage and stand in the joy of what is coming.

God, Please help everyone reading to catch the vision of being a massive, muscle-bound warrior. Help us grow mighty for battle in the power of the Holy Spirit. Thank You for the joy that comes from children following in truth.

~ Kimberlee Gill, academic dean

Clean Hearts

Create in me a clean heart, oh God; and renew a right spirit within me.

Psalm 51:10, KJV

~

In Psalm 51 we are allowed into a deeply personal moment between a man and his God. David, in deep repentance, decries his sin and requests God to transform the man that he is into the man God wants him to be.

Restoration of right love takes time.

In using the words create in me a clean heart, David acknowledges the need for something new. Even as lovers of God, we tend cling to the past and jointly love the wrong things as well. Our hearts affix to fleshly desires and worldly offerings. In my case, the pillow can call louder than the Sunday school class, the brownie louder than the celery, and the sarcastic comment louder and faster than the clamped lips. Sometimes, I even revel in the sin.

If it were just about me, things would look pretty bleak. But, we are blessed twofold to help us get our heart right: godly friends and a God Who desires us. After the sin of Bathsheba was pointed out to David by Namaan, he realized his heart's condition. Without Namaan, repentance may not have come. It is hard to appreciate those true friends in the moment they are revealing our sin, but it should be received in humility.

More amazing, remember it was God that sent Namaan to David. The Lord could have allowed David to continue in the sins and reap even more consequences, but instead He made opportunity for escape.

David's renewal was not a quick fix. Rather, he turned to God for a destroy and rebuild of his heart. Restoration of right love takes time, but David begged for and received opportunity for God's best.

Are you in sin? Know that you have hope in a Creator that believes you are worth the rebuild. He has called you to walk in fullness of joy.

God, I admit sometimes I think it would be easier to just be that robot in which I hand myself over and You program me just like You want. But in Your love, in Your mercy, You want all of me: spirit, mind, and body. I am sorry my mind and body are continual issues. Let my spirit rejoice in the beauty of holiness formed by You.

~ A teacher

Exuding Joy

Rejoice always, pray continually, give thanks in all circumstances;
for this is God's will for you in Christ Jesus.

I Thessalonians 5:16-18, NIV

~

The beginning of every school year is a special time for me. As I pray for my students by name, I feel so honored and blessed to be able to pour into their lives all year. I simply could not love them any more than if they were my very own children. My prayer is that they will learn to give thanks to the Lord in all circumstances as they consider the calling the Lord has placed on their life.

Teaching is my second profession, the profession through which the Lord has allowed me to experience a great amount of pure joy. High school students can be overwhelmed with the messages the world sends regarding money, success and self-importance. As a parent, I walked with my own children down this path and encouraged them to choose a profession that brought them pure joy, not a paycheck and not a title. Removing the stresses of what the world deems as successful allows the love of Jesus to shine through us and open doors to bring people to Christ.

> When money and worldly things become the primary focus, it is impossible to be joyful.

When our focus is living for the Lord and working to grow His kingdom, every other aspect of life falls into place. I have learned that The Lord will always provide, but we must teach children to live within our means. My children have seen what overextending financially can do to a family, and I try to share these lessons with my students as well. When money and worldly things become the primary focus, it is impossible to be joyful as a family. However, when living for Christ and serving Him in and through a chosen profession is the focus, the results are priceless.

Father God, I am so thankful that You are with us in all circumstances, for without You, we are nothing. We may not understand everything that we are experiencing; but Father, we know that with Your continuous love, all is well. I pray, Father God, that we all may seek Your will for our lives and let the worldly possessions go. Amen.

~ From the heart of the Utility Player, secondary science

Thankful Parenting

And whatever you do, whether in word or deed,
do it all in the name of the Lord Jesus,
giving thanks to God the Father through Him.
Colossians 3:17, NIV

Joint Heirs

And since we are his children, we are his heirs.
In fact, together with Christ we are heirs of God's glory.

Romans 8:17, NLT

~

As a Christian educator, I have a unique opportunity to show my students how valuable they are to God. Paul reminds us in this verse that all believers are God's children and have the same share in the blessings and sufferings of Christ himself. How unbelievable it is that God would treat us as equal to His own son. Maintaining this perspective in the classroom is not always easy. At home where you see all your children's flaws in 3D, it must be even harder. The good news is that God is offering your children exactly what every parent hopes for the very best He has to offer! We as parents and teachers have the opportunity to communicate this message to them.

Instill a sense of worth in my children.

Considering students to be my brothers and sisters fellow believers transforms the way I interact with them. Responding to their questions without rushing...and even pushing them to invest more in their studies are ways to show them that they are valuable. When I take this verse to heart, I experience compassion, forgiveness, and joy that I had not expected to find as a teacher of teenagers. Changing how I view the students changes me. In the classroom and at home, this verse is much like the Golden Rule for grown-ups. We teach our children from an early age to "do unto others," but do we follow suit? Do we manage to treat our children the way we want to be treated even as we teach and train them? Have we acknowledged them in our hearts to be joint heirs with Christ, our brothers and sisters?

Father, I am stunned that You look at me the same way You look at your son Jesus. Help me to instill a sense of worth in my children, and help them to value others in turn. May we consistently give thanks for all You have created us to be.

~ A. Gillespie, secondary English

God Provides

*And my God will meet all your needs according to the
riches of his glory in Christ Jesus.*

Philippians 4:19, NIV

~

I do not even want to know how much money my family has spent on tuition! Our oldest daughter started attending private Christian school in 1996. Then we added our middle daughter in 1998; and then our youngest graduated this year. We have spent a total of seventeen years of paying for Christian education for three daughters.

> ## Live with an eternal, rather than a worldly, perspective.

Although they have never told me so, I am sure that I have friends and family that think we have wasted our money through the years. But when asked if I think the sacrifice has been worth it, I respond with, "Yes, without a doubt!"

As I parent, I take Deuteronomy 6 very seriously. Regarding the commandments of God, we are to "…impress them on (our) children." It is hard to do that when the teachers are not allowed to teach with a biblical perspective. I am eternally grateful for the opportunity to have had godly teachers partner with my husband and me to consistently guide and teach our daughters to love and seek God with all that they are.

Has it been easy? Not at all. However, even through seasons of unemployment, God always provided what we needed to be able to keep our girls in a thoroughly Christian environment. God has taught us to be content with older, high-mileage vehicles, not eating out as much as we would like, and shopping at thrift stores in order to make ends meet. He has also taught us to live with an eternal, rather than worldly, perspective. We are grateful that God enabled us to make an eternal investment in our children.

Father God, thank You for providing for our every need as we seek to do Your will. Amen.

~ Judy Schmidt, teacher and junior high advisor

He's Mine

I am my beloved's, and his desire is toward me.

Song of Solomon 7:10, KJV

~

True confession. I am not always very loveable. My sisters would gladly share with you how I can be supremely bossy. My children know I have a temper. My husband sighs that I am a whiny wimp. (I make him hold my hand at the slightest medical discomfort, even during blood pressure checks.)

I am so thankful I belong to Him.

When I am at peak points in irritating mode, those who love me best stay clear; and I do not blame them. I am not proud of those moments, but they are a part of the me that I am working on.

At times, my flaws have brought rejection from those I love most. But then, there is my Jesus. He knows me best of all. He knows the roots of my sometimes ugly anger, the inside tears from fears of not being able to fix something. He knows when I am a complete mess. Still, his desire is towards me. Ask my Jesus, and He will always say, "She is my beloved."

My soul rejoices in my Savior, and I am so thankful I belong to Him.

Sweet Jesus, Thank You for Your deep, consuming love that wraps my soul in every moment of my life. I am a work in progress, and I fail in being the model of what You have called me to be. You love me anyway, and my soul is so grateful. I love You, too.

~ An educator and mother of three

Appointed Moments

~

It was May. My son's third season of college baseball was winding down. His team had advanced to the regional playoffs in Lubbock, Texas. He was slotted to pitch the first game of the tournament. Of course, this baseball mom was going to be at the biggest game of her son's baseball career. My daughter, on the other hand, was playing in her junior high soccer championship against a rival school. Of course, this soccer mom was not going to miss that event either! So, we stayed in Kansas City to watch the soccer championship victory. Although exhausted, we then drove many miles into Oklahoma before stopping for a brief night's rest. There are times when we do so much to encourage our children.

> God uses everything to bring about His purposes.

This is where our journey and this story take a detour. Her name was Olivia. I will never forget our encounter that May morning. She was a student at Texas Tech on her way home to Dallas. She had just finished finals, and we soon learned that she had not slept in about three days. On the highway in the middle of Texas, Olivia had fallen asleep while driving and crashed into a guardrail. When we came upon the accident, Olivia was on the ground. Her face was bleeding. We had a game to get to, but her need was great. So, we stopped the car and ran to her aid. My husband called 911, and my daughter provided ice from our cooler for her face. Then God just took over. I asked her name. Through her panic and tears, she told me that she was Olivia. I simply rubbed her back and asked if I could pray. She agreed, and God was present in that moment. When emergency workers arrived, we went on our way to the game. Our son pitched one inning, gave up two towering home runs and was done! This journey was not about supporting our son at all. It was about the God-appointed encounter with Olivia.

There are times when God does so much to encourage His children. I take joy in knowing He binds us together as one body, using our frailty to bring His strength in moments of need. I have learned in our submitted lives, God uses everything to bring about His purposes, even back-to-back games in different states.

Father, We need Your appointed moments to teach us how to better serve You. Help us to thankfully seize those moments so that we can teach our children to be Your hands and feet in this world. For in those moments, we can make a profound impact for You. Amen.

~ Michelle Bacon, fifth-grade teacher, mother of two

Live Desired

All Judah and Jerusalem mourned for Josiah. Then Jeremiah chanted a lament for Josiah. And all the male and female singers speak about Josiah in their lamentations to this day.

2 Chronicles 35:24-25

~

Live with an eternal, rather than worldly, perspective.

A strong tide of covenant breaking had swept through the land of Judah. One hundred years before Josiah took the throne, a momentary impediment to their idolatry had reigned under King Hezekiah. Judah wasted no time after his reign to clutch their disobedience. Yet, God in His mercy provided one more momentary curb in the face of Judah's self-wrought destruction: King Josiah.

When Josiah ascended the throne at age eight, it began a period during which God would encourage and strengthen his remnant before the coming judgment of Judah by way of Babylon. Josiah began with the repair and upkeep of the house of the Lord in the eighteenth year of His reign. During this process, the book of the law was discovered. Although the text does not share with us just how long God's people had been without the book of the law, it gives us tremendous insight through the statement of Shaphan in 2 Kings 22:10: "Hilkiah the priest has given me a book." God's people no longer recognized His Word.

In such an unfathomably dark time, God's Word was read to the king and the people, and it burst forth in glorious light and set the country ablaze with reformation. Josiah set about tearing down every false altar and ridding the people of every idol. He renewed the covenant between God and His people and did what was right in the sight of God. Upon his death the people mourned, and he filled their lamentations.

As we look at our own day through the lens of Josiah's Judah, we notice that we ourselves are in dark times. However, we also learn that these dark times were used for God's own ends and His church's good. In these times, will we forget God's Word and capitulate to the world or choose to stand?

Lord, You have permitted this time in our history to strengthen and encourage Your people to ready themselves to shine the light of the gospel. The world will not desire us or mourn our passing, but in doing all that is right in the sight of God, we will leave a sweet savor in the church. Through our testimony, many more may be drawn to our faithful Savior Jesus Christ. God, I am thankful for the opportunity to be an example for You.

~ Jacob Bluebaugh, resource services

Special Times

Now it came to pass, as they went, that he entered into a certain village: and a certain woman named Martha received him into her house. And she had a sister called Mary, which also sat at Jesus' feet, and heard his word. But Martha was cumbered about much serving, and came to him, and said, Lord, dost thou not care that my sister hath left me to serve alone? Bid her therefore that she help me. And Jesus answered and said unto her, Martha, Martha, thou art careful and troubled about many things: But one thing is needful: and Mary hath chosen that good part, which shall not be taken away from her.

Luke 10:38-42, KJV

~

Do you feel like your life is constantly busy? Sometimes working full-time, being a wife and a mom, I feel like I am not giving my best to each of these. I do not want my life to be so busy that I miss the special times.

Make time in your life for the special times.

God knew that my choosing to stay home from teaching a few years was what was best for our family. My grandma ended up getting really sick shortly after I began being home. I was able to help care for her and spend precious moments with her. I would not trade that time for anything. My grandma meant the world to me and to be able to spend those last few months with her was priceless. I will always remember her wanting to come with me to pick my son up from school and her insisting on taking the boys to Dairy Queen for an ice cream cone on the way home. These were special times I am glad I did not miss.

Now that I am back teaching, God daily reminds me to notice the special times throughout my day. It is a special time to walk my sons to their class each morning. It is a special time to say hi to them at lunch and see how their day is going. It is a special time to lie with them in their bed at night, even though there is laundry to be done and lunch to be made. I cherish those special times.

I challenge you to take time to make time in your life for the special times. Do not allow yourself to get so busy that you may miss them.

Jesus, Thank You for the special times in our lives that You give us. I pray that I will never take them for granted. Life is too short to be so busy. Thank You, Lord.

~ **Ashley Kates, fifth grade teacher, mom of two boys**

My Manna

He fed you with manna in the wilderness, a food unknown to your ancestors. He did this to humble you and test you for your own good.

Deuteronomy 8:16, NLT

~

As a mother of twins, my life can be hectic and full of stress. Sometimes I feel so run down because there is no break for me. I am Mom—24/7. I am Wife—24/7. I am many other titles and roles simultaneously. It is hard to stay on top of housework, my school work, teaching my children, cooking, and a million other things! The other day, I was lying in bed when I heard her sweet voice say "Mommy...." I went in and told her she needed to go to sleep like the rest of us, but I offered to rub her back and sing a lullaby. There was a sense of peace that came over me while singing to my sweet little girl. I saw her perfect face, remembering how she looked in the ultrasound pictures before she was born. I then had to think about the struggle just to have a child, much less twins.

We had been trying for over a year to conceive, and my doctor told me we most likely would not be able to get pregnant without help. I was devastated. We did not want to have to resort to fertility treatments if they could be avoided, so we went forward for prayer at our church on a Sunday morning. Around that same time, the conception of not just one baby, but two perfect babies was achieved. Not only were there two little miracles, but we had a boy and a girl. We had wanted two children, ideally wishing for a boy and a girl. God answered our prayers in His perfect way.

As I rubbed my daughter's back that night, I kept hearing, "This is my manna." When I thought back to Exodus, I remembered the story about manna. Although it was sent from heaven and was provided daily, the people began to get tired of the same old thing. They began to complain even though they were given everything they needed. How many times have I complained about my longed-for children? I must have read this verse many times before, but it never meant as much as when I read it this time.

Give God all the details that are too big for us to carry.

We must give God all the details that are too big for us to carry on our own. He never meant for us to do it alone. So let us give up the stress and be thankful for our manna!

God, in striving to be the best at all things for all people, I can feel overwhelmed and defeated. I am no good to anyone when I am full of stress and ready to blow at any moment. Please help me to please You and appreciate the "manna" with which You have so richly blessed me. Amen.

~ Jennie Schueller, fourth grade

Life in Death

For we who are alive are always being given over to death for Jesus' sake, so that his life may also be revealed in our mortal body. So then, death is at work in us, but life is at work in you.

II Corinthians 4:11-12, NIV

~

Sitting at a table of long-time members of ministry, I was struck by the level of pure exhaustion being described as each person made himself vulnerable to the like-minded group. It was a table of trusted friends. Battle stories and tears poured out. Being the youngest in the room, I stayed quiet and listened. Here were God's generals, pain and passion mingled within their words. Each had yielded a lifetime to support the causes of Christ. Like Paul, they recounted stories from the past years: financial pressures, gossips' division, co-leader moral failure, legal attack, family stress. They seemed "hard pressed on every side… perplexed…persecuted…and struck down" (II Corinthians 4:8).

My immaturity grasped for glory in the moment. These were God's best— where was the abundant blessing, cup runneth over, pressed down and shaken together stuff? Riches and a life of ease seemed more appropriate for this group. Hadn't my childhood lessons taught that when you choose the right path in life, you get happily ever after? My spirit cried out. "God, can't you see what your people have done for you? Lord, they suffer!" The Holy Spirit began hushing my mind, helping me to listen.

May our spirit control our minds and bodies.

The room turned to prayer and revealed depths of grace, wisdom, and gratitude. These warriors were not crushed nor in despair. They were not abandoned nor destroyed. They had joyfully exchanged the treasures of this world for the glories of His call. Yes, physical bodies were weakening, but their spirits were powerful! Their prayers rose in praise for souls that had been impacted and lives that had changed as a result of Christ's work through their submitted, gnarled hands of service. They were generals humble before their mighty King, and His glory was all around.

We are all members of ministry as we accomplish His work. May His spirit control our minds and bodies as we sometimes bemoan the great difficulty in the work of His kingdom. He did not promise the ministry would be easy, but we can trust it is gloriously eternal.

Lord, I can be such a whiner. I want to serve You, but I forget sometimes that this is a war we are fighting. Today, I am thankful You are willing to tear down my flesh with its selfish desires and replace it with a spirit that hungers and thirsts after You. Thank You for those that have suffered before me so that I could come to know You more. Help me to lay down my life for the cause of Christ.

~ **A growing educator, momma of three**

Total Praise

I lift up my eyes to the hills—where does my help come from?
My help comes from the LORD, the Maker of heaven and earth.

Psalm 121:1-2, NIV

~

Being completely surrendered to God is one of my ultimate desires.

This passage of Scripture has been set to music many times over the years, but one of my favorites has to be Richard Smallwood's version. In this particular song, the lyrics continue, "You are the source of my strength, You are the strength of my life, I lift my hands in total praise to You."[7] Total…praise.

I have seen people emphatically lift their hands for a variety of reasons: the batter hits a home run, the police officer commands it, the band begins playing their number one hit, and a student knows the answer to the question. But the act of lifting one's hands in total praise to God is truly an act of complete surrender.

Being completely surrendered to God is one of my ultimate desires for the children and students God has entrusted to me. As I have played this song on full blast in the family van, and as I have taught it to my choirs, I have been careful to emphasize the importance is complete surrender – not the act of lifting their hands. I want them to complete their homework, clean their rooms, play sports, perform in music and drama, serve others, pray, give, and work at their jobs with total praise. We should live surrendered lives in response to our maker and all He has done for us. We should live our lives in total praise.

Father, Thank You for all You have done and continue to do to cause us to praise You. May the actual or figurative lifting of our hands show our complete surrender to You.

~ Trissa Lucht, choir teacher

Heavenly Peace

"For my thoughts are not your thoughts, neither are your ways my ways,"
declares the Lord. "As the heavens are higher than the earth, so are my ways
higher than your ways and my thoughts than your thoughts."

Isaiah 55:8-9, NIV

~

As a mom holding my newborn son, I offered up many prayers of praise and thankfulness. Some prayers were general and others were more specific. Ultimately, I wanted my child to be happy and follow God's will for his life. I prayed specifically and repeatedly that God would never send this precious gift to war—my thoughts and my ways.

However, the Lord had a specific plan for my son and began to reveal it while he was still in high school. Although he was not a typical candidate, God was purposefully calling him to United States Military Academy at Westpoint. When he began to reveal what he thought God's plan was for his life, my heart sank. I prayed that he would never go to war, yet God was calling him to prepare for just that calling. Thankfulness escaped me.

> As God was working on my son's heart, he was also working on mine.

As God was working on my son's heart, he was also working on mine. My husband and I raised our children to be aware of God's calling on their heart, so we scheduled a tour and headed east. I will never forget that turning moment when we were on campus: 4,000 cadets were lined up for lunch at the mess hall, bells were tolling "On Christ the Solid Rock I Stand" across campus, and I felt complete peace. At the same time, I received a text from my son who was at a different location on campus but heard the same song. He also felt peace that this was exactly where God wanted him to be.

Our joy as parents in that moment was the realization that our son was listening to God, and His plan was solidified in all of our hearts. Often, parents have grand plans for their children and do everything possible to secure the future they think is best for their families. Yet, our Heavenly Father, Who knows the number of hairs on our head, in His divine sovereignty, has mapped out His plan for our lives. That knowledge brings a thankfulness and peace that passes all understanding.

Lord God, I praise You for Your sovereignty. Though I confess to You the desires of my heart, please continue to prepare my heart for Your perfect will in my life and in the lives of my children. Thank You for working Your perfect will in us. In Your sacred name, Amen.

~ From the heart of Sue Santon, teacher

Important Possessions

Do not lay up for yourselves treasures on earth, where moth and rust destroy and where thieves break in and steal; but lay up for yourselves treasures in heaven, where neither moth nor rust destroys and where thieves do not break in and steal. For where your treasure is, there your heart will be also.

Matthew 6:19-20, NKJV

~

What is your most treasured possession? What could you not live without in your household? Microwave? Large, flat screen, plasma TV? Computer? Smartphone? iPad? Recently my Spanish 2 classes were practicing speaking about household and personal possessions. We classified objects as necessities or luxuries. I asked them this question expecting typical teenage material possessions as answers. I was totally blown away by their responses. The first student said, "my mother." That should have clued me in to their mindset, but I said it could not be a person, it had to be a thing. The next student said, "my home and my family." (Wow!) I called on one more student, who said, "the Bible." At this point, I stopped asking questions and told them how impressed I was by their responses.

Have a heart to teach what God thinks is important.

I am not a novice teacher. I literally have decades of experience teaching in a public high school, but this is my first year in private Christian education. This was not the first time I had asked questions like this. The usual responses were cell phone, car, or computer. What makes these students so different? The answer is that they are surrounded by people who have a heart to teach them what God thinks is important. Your children are learning the most important lessons in life, and they have been learning them first of all from you, their parents.

Heavenly Father, Thank You so much for blessing these children with parents who know You, love You, and strive to follow Your will in raising them. Thank You also for the awesome and rewarding experience of being a part of Your plan in their lives.

~ **Cheryl Patneau, high school foreign language**

Never Broken

"Just as I swore in the time of Noah that I would never again let a flood cover the earth and destroy its life, so now I swear that I will never again pour out my anger on you. For the mountains may depart and the hills disappear, but even then I will remain loyal to you. My covenant of blessing will never be broken," says the Lord, who has mercy on you.

Isaiah 4:9-10, NLT

~

Everyone knows that the rainbow means God promised to never again destroy the earth. However, were you aware that He made an equally binding promise and even used His "rainbow promise" as a mnemonic that He would never again pour out His anger?

His provision and His pardon are so perfect.

You might be thinking: "So let me get this straight…. God made a covenant that he will NEVER again pour out his anger on me? And this covenant will never be broken? Huh? …So God isn't mad at me?"

That's right. God is not mad at you. I do not know about you, but this verse was a revelation to me. I mean, don't you know, we have all sinned and fallen short of the glory of God? (Romans 3:23). And if you did not remember that lately, sometimes there are plenty of people around to remind you. Funny, people have no trouble remembering that one.

Of course, I had heard the ol' 'there is now no condemnation for those who are in Christ…' (Romans 8:1, NIV) many times, but somehow it did not send a lightning bolt through my spirit to my heart like this truth did. God is not mad at me. God isn't mad at me. Just repeat it a few times till it really sticks in your own heart…or better yet, open up His Word and read it for yourself. It's right there…promise! So my challenge to you is this: The next time you see lightning, remember God is NOT mad at you!

He abundantly provides mercy. In fact, His provision and His pardon are so perfect that it says in Hebrews 10:14 "for by that one offering he perfected forever all those whom He is making holy." In verse 17, "I will never again remember their sins and lawless deeds." Not only are we forgiven, but He chooses to think about us as if we had never sinned at all!

Heavenly Father, Thank You for sending Jesus to die in my place. Thank You for forgiving me of my sins and choosing to instantly forget them. Thank You, Jesus, for taking all the anger that should have been mine and bearing it yourself in my stead. Help me to live in light of this truth and to shine brightly for You. Help me keep this promise in mind when someone disappoints me. Help me to remember to walk in love and not in anger. Amen.

~ An educator

Praying Parents

That our sons may be as plants grown up in their youth;
That our daughters may be as pillars, sculptured in palace style.

Psalm 144:12, NKJV

~

Full-grown plants have roots that ground them and growth that bears fruit. Pillars connect the walls of a building with the cornerstone; and when they are sculpted in palace style, they are beautiful! Isn't this what we want for our sons and daughters? I sure did.

As the winds blow, they are immovable.

Adolescence has always been thought of as that time between childhood and adulthood, normally thought of as the teen years. It's a time of transition towards maturity. But now we live in a world where researchers are saying adolescence lasts until age 28! The last thing we want is a bunch of twenty-somethings still living at home and still being supported by mom and dad. The trend is towards the unstable, unconnected, unproductive twenty-year-olds who are still trying to figure themselves out. Raising children in the current culture is not for the faint of heart.

I often prayed that my sons would be mature, grounded, followers of Christ, bearing fruit while they were still young. I prayed that the way they interact with others, the decisions they make, their actions and their responses would be mature ones. Now that they are grown, I am thankful to attest to the faithfulness of God in His answer to my prayer.

And now I have granddaughters, and I get to pray the second half of the verse. I pray that they will be the connector, the stabilizer, the one holding fast to the chief cornerstone. I pray they stand straight and strong and know that they are beautiful because they were fearfully and wonderfully made. I pray that nothing rocks their world. As the winds blow, they are immovable.

Dear Lord, Your Word is a lamp unto my feet and a light unto my path. I know it doesn't return void. I pray now for our sons, that they be mature while in their youth. Help them to escape the culture of today that tells them to reject responsibility. Help them to be rooted in You and let them bear fruit. I pray too for our daughters to stand tall, confident that they are beautifully and skillfully created and connected to You, the chief cornerstone. Let them stabilize their families and all those around them.

~ Linda Harrelson, head of school

Perfect Children

Behold, children are a heritage from the Lord, The fruit of the womb is a reward.

Psalm 127:3, NKJV

~

Teacher conferences are always an interesting time. What a joy it is to partner with families in bringing their children to their potential in Christ! I can tell so many stories of laughing, crying, and praying with parents. And, as all teachers, I can tell stories of conferences where I went home and wept.

There are no perfect children.

Hardest of all for me is when I have a child who tries but just cannot produce grades that parents find acceptable. Here is my secret: I hate grades. People think they tell the whole story, and they most certainly do not. Through the years, I have had parents able to express only disappointment once their eyes land on the report card and narrow in on that column of letters. Despite my words of praise, I can see that for some, only the grade column matters.

I want to encourage parents, every child is a reward from the Lord. You can be thankful for each one the Lord has given to you! As your child's teacher, I do not have a grade column for purity of heart, empathy, creativity, or ability to demonstrate servant leadership. Please remember, the grade column is an indicator of current academic understanding in a given subject area. It is not a guarantee for future success or God's ability to use them in a mighty way!

Parents, join with me in rejoicing in your child's giftings. We can partner together to keep the academics moving up; but if you can only express disappointment to your child, it makes the academic learning even harder.

Together, let us be thankful for each gift within the amazing children the Lord has allowed us to mentor. There are no perfect children, but our perfect Lord has designed each one for a distinct purpose that fits His plan as they walk toward perfection in Him.

Heavenly Father, Thank You for the reward of my children. I am honored to have been entrusted to lead them according to Your plans. Always let my face, my mouth, and my actions lead them to greater knowledge of who they are in You!

~ A veteran in love with kids

Empty Nest

Because of the Lord's great love we are not consumed, for his compassions never fail. They are new every morning; great is your faithfulness.

Lamentations 3: 22-23, NIV

~

It is May 10, 2013. Grandparents, aunts, uncles, cousins, and out-of-town guests are visiting. The bakery cake has been purchased, the punch bowl brought up from the basement, and the house is cleaner than it has been in some time. I drove to school alone today for the first time in years. You see my youngest daughter will graduate this evening. After sixteen years of bringing a daughter to work with me, I will now come alone.

> **But I know that I can trust my God Who is faithful.**

I have never welcomed change. God exercised his sense of humor when he placed my husband Leroy and I together. Leroy loves change: change of the furniture arrangement, change cars, change clothes, change jobs, and on and on. I, however, would be happy living in the same predictable routine the rest of my life! I lived in the same house all of my childhood until I graduated from college. So God (and Leroy) has had to push me to try new things, change up the routine, and even to go back to school to try a new profession.

So, am I anxious about being an empty nester and having to be content with the changes in my life? Absolutely! But I know that I can trust my God, Who is faithful to guide and equip me through all of the changes that lie ahead.

Father God, I thank You that You are with me every step of the way through this life, whether it be mundane and routine or exciting and changing. Amen.

~ Judy Schmidt, teacher and junior high advisor

Legacy

Likewise urge the young men to be sensible, in all things show yourself to be an example of good deeds, with purity in doctrine, dignified, sound in speech which is beyond reproach, so that the opponent will be put to shame, having nothing bad to say about us.

Titus 2:6-8, NASB

~

I do not know that I realized the full impact of my father's example until I moved out. Prior to spreading my wings, I noticed his example and appreciated his solidarity in integrity, but I did not genuinely grasp the impact of his character upon his peers or me. It did not require a large sum of time for the Lord to impress upon me the incredible gift I had been granted in my father.

Recent times have shown a waning of earnest and godly examples for young men and women. The generations present before us are plagued by vague doctrine, irregular church concern, infidelity, dishonesty, and indifference. With such a dizzying spectacle of inconsistency, it is no wonder that our young ones flounder through their teenage and early adult years; they have not seen or been taught how to begin or finish the race.

> Right doctrine informs right practice.

Here, Paul writes to Titus and prescribes how the younger men, and indeed young people in general, are to learn their roles as future torchbearers. Paul exhorts the older men to set the example in conduct, speech, deeds, and doctrine. Importantly, doctrine is maintained in the list that otherwise focuses on conduct. Right orthodoxy informs right orthopraxy; right doctrine informs right practice. Without a firm grasp of the gospel and God's revelation to man through Scripture, our conduct cannot be rightly aligned to God's standards; instead, it becomes a game of preferences.

In Proverbs 22:6 we are instructed to train children in the manner in which they should go before the Lord. This should not be understood solely as head knowledge, but should also be comprised of the example we set for our children. It is one thing to tell our children that they should behave and think in a certain manner, but it is another to behave and think in that manner in our own walk. Through our example, we show our heart to our children.

Lord, before You I ask, am I setting the example of good works? Am I maintaining a purity of doctrine before the ever-watching eyes of the world? Lord, I desire my speech and conduct to be such that the world can bring no true accusation against me. Allow my children to have cause for thanks in the example I bring.

~ Jacob Bluebaugh, resource services

Testimony

Yet I will rejoice in the Lord, I will joy in the God of my salvation.

Habbakuk 3:18 NIV

~

At the age of eight, my good buddy Rocky invited me to come to a children's crusade at his church. I had never been to church before, but the crusade promised to be great fun. Singing cowboys, games, prizes, and a lot of other kids were promised. I had no idea what I was signing up for, but I was in!

But I know that I can trust my God Who is faithful.

The crusade lasted an entire week; and around day three, I knew I wanted to ask Jesus to come into my heart. I saw the joy around me; I felt loved by everyone I met. When the cowboy asked kids to come to the altar if they wanted to pray, I ran!

I let my mom know that I would be needing to go to Sunday school, and that I had signed up for the Sunday school bus. She was all for putting me on the bus, along with my younger sisters. When we were in church, she got to have a Sunday morning in peace.

The Sunday school bus came with a Saturday surprise. How I loved Leonard, my Sunday school bus driver. He would come by on Saturdays and talk to us about Jesus. When we realized Leonard would come every Saturday, we started gathering friends in the neighborhood to listen to his Bible stories. Then Sunday mornings, he would pull up, and out we would run.

Only a short year later, my entire family was in church. A year after that it was my dad helping Leonard drive the Sunday school bus. Now forty years down life's road, I have opportunity to minister to students every day, passing on a little of Rocky, the cowboy crusader, Leonard, my parents, and the many people who showed me Jesus along the way.

Joyful, joyful, God, I adore You. Your love, through Your people, saved me.

Jesus, in this fallen world, call us to minister to Your people. Father, please allow the joy of Your salvation to bubble over onto the lost world around us. Even now, Lord, call forth cowboy crusaders, bus drivers, and laborers for Your harvest.

~ Kimberlee Gill, academic dean

Great Sacrifice

For God so loved the world so much that he gave his one and only Son, so that everyone who believes in him will not perish but have eternal life.

John 3:16, NLT

~

I recall the struggle to become pregnant. A lot of prayer and miracles led to the conception and birth of my twins. While approximately seven months pregnant, I was in a horrible car accident. I had been stopped on a highway for a funeral procession when someone came over a hill going 65-70 mph and hit the back of my car. I remember screaming aloud, "Oh God, Oh God, Oh God!" It was a prayer cried out of pure terror that did not cease from my lips until well after the car had stopped. Contractions immediately began, and I was rushed to the hospital. In the ambulance, I was petrified because the enemy was attacking my emotions by reminding me that the seatbelt was right on my lower stomach where my daughter was located. I felt fear overcoming me, so I quickly began to ask God to help me remain calm. I took slow deep breaths while praying so my babies' stress would be lessened. I began standing on the promise that God works out everything for the good of those who love Him. He had just performed the miracle of helping us get pregnant, so I trusted He would save my babies. I had to be on bed rest from October to December, waiting for the perfect day when my babies were eventually born. They arrived safe and healthy. God saved us.

> I am redeemed by the ultimate price and sacrifice.

As I held them, I reflected on Mary with Jesus. I understood as never before the magnitude of the sacrificed Son. I had been holding my children only for a short time, and I was overwhelmed at the idea of Mary as she watched her promise from God be nailed on a cross. I thought of the heavenly Father's surrender of His only Son for my sins. I am redeemed by the ultimate price and sacrifice.

A challenge for those of us who have heard John 3:16 quoted throughout our lives is to not become desensitized to the message of the cross: there was an ultimate sacrifice that saved us. The Father, Mary, Jesus--all endured immeasurable agony for us.

Meditate on God giving His only Son to save us. Then, wholeheartedly offer Him Thanks.

Heavenly Father, Thank You for sacrificing Your beloved Son for me. Help me to really understand what that sacrifice means and be thankful that You felt we all are worthy of being Your children. I love You, Father. In Jesus' name, Amen.

~ Mrs. Schueller, fourth grade

Grace-filled Parenting

But by the grace of God I am what I am: and his grace
which was bestowed upon me was not in vain;
but I labored more abundantly than they all: yet
not I, but the grace of God which was with me.
I Corinthians 15:10, KJV

Falling Down

Two people are better off than one, for they can help each other succeed. If one person falls, the other can reach out and help. But someone who falls alone is in real trouble.

Ecclesiastes 4:9-10, NLT

~

Many times as a teacher I have gotten in my car to leave for the day, closed the door, and started to cry. Sometimes I am just tired and stressed. Sometimes I am responding to bad news about a student or staff member's family. Just as often, though, I cry because I have witnessed a student face a challenge—academic, moral, or personal—and fail. I hurt for them when they struggle to grasp a concept we are studying, or when they make poor choices, or when they suffer the consequences of those choices. I am certain that you as a parent grieve much more than I do when your child fails. So what do we do?

They must witness us humbly admit to and face our mistakes.

We can relate to them. All adults have experienced moments of failure, and taking a moment to share one of those experiences with your children may remind them that they are not alone. If nothing else, recalling our own experiences may help us to tap into compassion and sympathy. We can also remind our children that Christ redeems our errors and makes all things new. He is a God of second chances. "God sent His Son into the world not to judge the world, but to save the world through Him. There is no judgment against anyone who believes in Him'" (John 3:17-18, NLT). God forgives our mistakes and continues to view us as his children and not as failures. Our children will have to face the consequences of their mistakes, but we can walk with them through it. They must also see evidence that the "godly may trip seven times, but they get up again" (Proverbs 24:16, NLT). As we lead by example, they must witness us humbly admit to and face our mistakes.

Thank You, God, that You put people in my life to pick me up when I fall. When my children make mistakes, help me to demonstrate love and compassion rather than anger. I want to show them how to honor You even in difficult situations.

~ A. Gillespie, secondary English

Got Grace

But by the grace of God I am what I am, and His grace toward me did not prove vain; but I labored even more than all of them, yet not I, but the grace of God with me.

I Corinthians 15:10, NASB

~

Ever had one of those mornings where you just did not want to get up? Maybe you had that feeling the entire day. Maybe it was a season of life where you lacked motivation to do the right thing. What's the answer? Grace.

In the classroom too, the best motivator is not candy, money, or bonus points. It is grace. Everybody likes a little grace because everyone is a sinner. Students like grace. However, as a teacher, how do I find the right balance between giving grace and maintaining high standards? I believe it is all in the approach.

I try not to give in but rather "grace in."

Grace can most fairly and significantly be given to students, based on a teacher's approach. For example, when a student makes the same mistake again for the seventeenth time on his or her homework, it is not time to give up. It is time to "grace up." By this, I don't mean the student gets 100% because it is clear he or she will never get it. A "grace up" in teaching is when you let a student know you accept him or her as a person, even though you know with little doubt his or her struggle will likely never go away completely.

As a teacher, I try not to give in but rather "grace in." Not give up, but rather "grace up." I maintain the standard but let the students know that I accept them in grace, even if it takes them ninety-three times to hit the standard.

Perhaps this is what Christian education is all about.

Dear Great Grace-Giver, Help me show Your grace in the way I interact with students that parents have loaned to me for that moment at school. Help the students to know that I will accept them in grace while I still maintain the high standard of excellence. Help me to teach them by word and deed to be motivated by Your grace in Jesus Christ!

~ Six-year educator

Opportunity

Today I have given you the choice between life and death, between blessings and
curses. Now I call on heaven and earth to witness the choice you make.
Oh, that you and your descendants might live! You can make this choice by
loving the Lord your God, obeying him, and committing yourself firmly to him.
This is the key to your life. And if you love and obey the Lord, you will live long
in the land the Lord swore to give your ancestors Abraham, Isaac, and Jacob.

Deuteronomy 30:19-20, NLT

~

In the midst of raw emotion, we must pause to seek the way.

As I picked up my children from my mom's house after work, she proceeded to tell me about something special that had happened that day. She said that my son had come to her saying, "Nana, do you want Jesus to live in my heart?" She said, "Yes, but do you want Jesus to live in your heart?" He replied, "Yes." She was then able to pray with him the prayer of salvation at the age of four. I exulted to know that my son had chosen Christ as his Savior. It was not complicated. He simply wanted Jesus to live in his heart.

I considered what may have happened if my son had been in a different place at the time of his inquiry. What if he were attending a school where a teacher would not have wanted or been able to pray with him? What if my mom would have dismissed his desires as naivety because of his age?

These questions led me to think about missed opportunities. How many times in our life does God present us a pivotal moment? Do we recognize in the moment the choices that could bring either life or death? It is hard to think that we would ever choose curses or choose to miss God-given opportunities, but our actions may reflect otherwise. In every decision, there is a choice to do things God's way or the way that leads to brokenness. In the midst of raw emotion, we must pause to seek the way that leads to life.

God, Thank You for my son's salvation; and my mother's pause to take opportunity.
Lord, I do not want to miss opportunities that You have designed for my life path.
Please forgive me for overlooking them or choosing the wrong way. Please lead me in
every part of my life and enable me to lead others as You would have them go. Lord, I
long to walk only in Your grace. In Jesus' name.

~ Mrs. Schueller, fourth grade

Competition Compromise

Do you not know that in a race all the runners run, but only one gets the prize? Run in such a way as to get the prize. Everyone who competes in the games goes into strict training. They do it to get a crown that will not last, but we do it to get a crown that will last forever. Therefore I do not run like someone running aimlessly; I do not fight like a boxer beating the air. No, I strike a blow to my body and make it my slave so that after I have preached to others, I myself will not be disqualified for the prize.

I Corinthians 9:24-27, NIV

~

In a world of competitive sports, where kids are beginning to compete as young as two years old, sometimes we have a hard time drawing the line of an appropriate level of competition. Where does their competitive spirit come from? Are children born with the drive, or do they inherit the competitive spirit from their parents?

To try and make that distinction, I like to paint a mental picture of Jesus by thinking, "What would Jesus look like if He were called to be a soccer player?"

> Live as children of the light.

- He would give 100% effort every time whether practice or a game. Col. 3:23
- His goal scoring celebration would be giving the glory to God. 1 Cor. 10:31
- He would follow the rules of the game and gracefully respect the referees. Titus 3:1
- He would encourage his teammates in the good and bad times. Heb. 3:13
- His actions on and off the field would let others clearly see His faith. 2 Tim. 2:15

Do you compromise your grace and integrity for competition in a game? Does the light of Christ shine through you for all to see on and off the field? In I Corinthians 11:1, we are called to imitate Christ and to live as children of the light. If you call yourself a Christian, the actions that take place on the field are painting a picture for others. What kind of picture are you painting?

Jesus, Thank You for living a grace-filled life that we can use as an example of how to live. Thank You for the joyfulness that we get by playing and watching sports. Help my light to shine grace in all circumstances so that I can help paint a clear picture of Who You are. Amen.

~ Coach "Ammo" Siemsen, PE teacher & soccer coach

Clay Pots II

*For God, who said, "Let there be light in the darkness," has made this
light shine in our hearts so we could know the glory of God that is seen in the
face of Jesus Christ. We now have this light shining in our hearts, but
we ourselves are like fragile clay jars containing this great treasure.*

II Corinthians 4:7, NLT

~

First problem with clay pots: they are fragile. It is so easy to crack or chip them. If you drop one, chances are it will shatter into a million pieces. Second problem with clay pots: when they break they make a mess and cleaning up the breakage can be dangerous! Have you ever cut yourself trying to deal with a broken glass in a sink of soapy water?

We forget our own jagged edges are sticking out.

Sometimes living in the Body of Christ can be as hazardous as fishing broken shards of glass out of murky water. It is not that we mean to snag or cut each other. We are just so focused on trying to dodge everyone else's broken places (and super glue our own shattered pieces) that we forget our own jagged edges are sticking out and impaling our hapless neighbors!

We like to say we are "under construction" when we want others to overlook the damage our brokenness inflicts. When other people's jagged edges stab us, however, we are not as inclined to chalk the injury up to the standard risks of negotiating construction sites. Make no mistake, I Peter 2 reminds us that we "like living stones, are being built into a spiritual house."

Jesus, We know You are the cornerstone. Cover our brokenness so we do not endanger our fellow workers. Give us Your grace to maneuver the broken edges of others. When the process gets messy and jagged edges cut us, help us trust Your vision for the temple you're building. Give us Your grace to maneuver the broken edges of others.

~ Mrs. Terry, secondary history

No Worries

Whatever you do, work at it with all your heart,
as working for the Lord, not for human masters.

Colossians 3:23, KJV

~

There are few things in life that give me more pleasure than knowing I have accomplished something in an excellent manner. Lest I sound completely pompous, I firmly acknowledge this accomplishment most certainly is not a reflection of me, but rather of the Christ in me. A quote from Erma Bombeck has been a life mantra. She said, "When I stand before God at the end of my life, I would hope that I would not have a single bit of talent left, and could say, 'I used everything You gave me.'"[8] Even as I write now, the words are the tearful cry of my soul. I want to be God's Colossians 3:23 girl.

As you can imagine, with a steady drive to perform, I strive constantly for personal balance and must intentionally work not to drive everyone crazy with to-do lists.

> In two words I felt empowered, affirmed, and inspired.

In growing me along, God, in His faithfulness, has provided a friend who poured grace out on me in abundance. She did it with two simple words, "No worries." As I would race by or into her office, I would frequently mention something I knew she needed from me but had not gotten to yet. Her reply was always with a smile, "No worries."

Unbelievable to me was the soothing power of those two little words. They were a balm of Gilead to my racing mind. I did not need to stress; she knew I was on it. The words meant everything was ok! Life is good and to be enjoyed! In two words I felt empowered, affirmed, and inspired to a higher calling: peace.

In my job I have learned that there are many people who can get a lot of things done and do them well. But, to be a person who can bring grace and peace to others? Now that is something to strive for.

Lord, I thank You for the good work You have set before us to do! What a joy to get to help out in the kingdom! But right now, Lord, I give special thanks for Your design of peace that is promised to us as we go about Your work. I know the message of peace is all over Your Word. Thank You so much for being an amazing God who provides fellow laborers to be Your Living Word in the middle of our rush for You. God, I am asking You to help me be a peace giver. Let my words be filled with the grace that can only come from being intimate with You. Lord, let me inspire rather than agitate! My heart wants only to please You.

~ An educating "Martha"

Mind Molding

We now have this light shining in our hearts, but we ourselves are like fragile clay jars containing this great treasure. This makes it clear that our great power is from God, not from ourselves. We are pressed on every side by troubles, but we are not crushed. We are perplexed, but not driven to despair. We are hunted down, but never abandoned by God. We get knocked down, but we are not destroyed.

II Corinthians 4:7-9, NLT

~

To do what daily life demands does not come from me.

During my first year of teaching, I had a student who was a sweet and charming child. Despite these qualities, he often made negative statements about himself. He would use phrases like, "I'm stupid. I hate my brain." This was, of course, alarming as his teacher. Why did not this wonderful little boy understand that people don't always make perfect choices? Why did not he realize his worth and how great he was? Did he know that I still cared about him even though I was upset by his choices? I could not let the negative words weigh upon him without having a one-on-one discussion. My words to him were unforgettable, not because they were intellectually stimulating, but because God used those very words to speak to my own heart. "I think you're great! It makes me sad to hear you say bad things about yourself. You are an amazing little boy! You need to be nice to yourself. Can you try to say good things next time?" He agreed, and his attitude did change for the better throughout the school year.

How many times does the God who knows my every thought wish I would be nicer to myself? I bet it hurts my Creator to hear my thoughts and sometimes spoken, negative remarks. "I'm such a bad mother! Why am I distracted by everything going on? I'm not strong enough. Why did God bless me with children if He knew I would struggle so much in being good enough for them?" I wonder if God sees something in me like I saw in my student? My words to him were a revelation God sent right back to me.

I am challenged to remember that the great power to do what daily life demands does not come from me, but from Him. Because of Him, we are not crushed. We are not driven to despair. We are never abandoned by God. We are not destroyed. Take heart in those words and be nice to yourself...God thinks you are great!

continued

God, You know my insecurities. You formed me and know exactly where I struggle daily. I feel like a frequent failure, but I know Your Word says I am more than a conqueror. I can do all things through Christ. I ask that You help me be the mother You want me to be. Help me to be nice to myself and to get back up when I fall. It is an insult to You when I constantly speak negative words over myself. Help me, God. I love You and thank You for every eye-opening moment. In Jesus' Name.

~ Jennie Schueller, fourth-grade teacher

Girl Drama

*Do nothing out of selfish ambition or vain conceit, but in humility
consider others better than yourselves.*

Philippians 2:3, NIV

~

A few "open-toe shoe" seasons ago, a Facebook friend posted a status on her
wall about seeing someone out shopping wearing flip-flops without a pedicure.
After posting her disgust, she was quickly backed up by a slew of agreeing
commenters. I found myself feeling quite inferior all of a sudden, as I was
sporting comfy flip-flops myself and never gave a
second thought to other people looking at my feet
when I am standing in line at the store.

Look past our labels and logos and encourage each other.

Such simple judgmentalism is the root of much girl
drama. We make comparisons that come from our
natural (sinful) nature that divide us into groups
and establish the social pecking order. Women with
painted toenails are clearly "better than" women who
do not have painted, soft feet, right?! Designer jeans
and handbags, name brand clothing, cars we drive…
the list could go on. Where do our daughters learn
to compare themselves to others? They learn this
skill from us, of course. Have you ever found yourself
shopping at Wal-Mart but considered yourself in a
class above other Wal-Mart shoppers? Women, we need to check ourselves.
God does not ask us not to enjoy nice things, but in our culture we have to be
very careful that we are not idolizing the idea of our image.

I admit, I am as guilty as the next person. Will you join me as I strive to impart
truth to my daughters, and yours, about who they are in Christ? We are
beautiful, valuable creations of the God of the universe. Let us look past our
labels and logos and encourage each other with wisdom, and Truth, building
each other up from the inside out. If that involves making a date for a pedicure,
let us do that, too!

*Father God, Thank You for entrusting two beautiful girls to me. I am constantly
humbled by all that You teach me through them. Please help us all to strive to be more
like You and less like the world as we teach and train our daughters and interact with
each other. Amen.*

~ **Trish Teilborg, early elementary teacher**

Real Life

Your own ears will hear him. Right behind you a voice will say, "This is the way you should go," whether to the right or to the left.

Isaiah 30:21, NLT

~

Shortly after I married (and acquired two boys on the honeymoon), I realized I was totally unqualified for this parenting gig. I remember sitting in the dark crying and wondering whether I had been mistaken when I thought God told me to marry the older man with kids. After all, I was not even going to church; how could I be certain? Was it fair to saddle these two little guys with a stepmom who had never even babysat? (To make matters worse, I had opted for tutoring rather than babysitting because I did not really like kids, even when I was one.)

> With His grace, I could bear the challenges.

I came disturbingly close to packing a bag and running for the hills. You know what stopped me? I had read somewhere that children often blame themselves when their parents split up. (Now, I have no idea whether or not what I read was accurate; so please don't let an article I read 30+ years ago trigger a guilt trip if you have experienced a divorce.) That is not the point, this is: I stayed.

A few months later, we surrendered our lives to God; and no, things did not magically improve overnight. This was real life, not a Disney movie. There were still days when I wanted to run. Nothing has brought me to my knees in repentance and desperation more than marriage and parenting. At critical points, I often heard His voice letting me know the way to go. He was with me and with His grace, I could bear the challenges.

Together marriage and parenting have been the most difficult, confusing, humbling, and stressful jobs I've ever undertaken. They have also been the most rewarding. Bob and I will be celebrating our 37th anniversary in June 2015.

Thank You, Lord, for the indescribable blessing of children and the wonderful messes and challenges they bring. We are so grateful that You do not expect us to figure it out by ourselves. We need to hear You in our own ears, not second-hand. Give us ears to hear and courage to stay the course when the answers do not come quickly.

~ **Mrs. Terry, secondary history**

Worn Down

Come to me, all you who are weary and burdened, and I will give you rest.

Matthew 11:28, NIV

~

But I know that I can trust my God Who is faithful.

Do you feel worn? Do you feel tattered? Do you feel defeated with the battles of life? It is hard to pick yourself up some days or some moments when you do not have much to give. It is easy to put a happy face on for the world to see, but deep down you are overwhelmed, overworked, and heavy-hearted. There are typically two ways that we as humans try to slap the band-aid on to help us heal. The first way is to go talk to someone about what is going on and receive encouragement to "refuel" our energy and mindset. The second way is to face and fight the battle on our own. Have you noticed that Christ is not in that picture?

Not only does He say to come to Him when we are weary and burdened, but the Lord talks about how He delights in us when we are weak. It is hard to feel delightful when you are weak, but the Lord looks at you and smiles because this is when Christ's power is made perfect in you. It does not matter how deep you are buried in the quicksand of your busy life, Christ himself delights in you…in weakness, in insults, in hardships, in persecutions, in difficulties…rely on Him and rejoice in your weakness for Christ will use you in some powerful way.

"But He said to me, 'My grace is sufficient for you, for my power is made perfect in weakness.' Therefore I will boast all the more gladly about my weaknesses, so that Christ's power may rest on me. That is why, for Christ's sake, I delight in weaknesses, in insults, in hardships, in persecutions, in difficulties. For when I am weak, then I am strong" (II Corinthians 12: 9-10, NIV).

He alone can give true peace to your burdensome heart. Go to your Heavenly Father. He is calling you. He wants to hear from you when you are worn, tattered, or defeated with battles of life. Tell Him everything that is going on, and He will guard your heart and your mind in Him.

Lay everything at the feet of Christ, and you will find your rest. What is holding you back?

Lord, Give me strength in this time of weakness and overwhelming amounts of work. I know in James it talks about considering all trials and tribulations joy. Lord, You are my joy. Because of You, I know that I will be used in some powerful way. Thank You for the rest and the peace that You give my heart, soul, and mind. I love You. Amen.

~ Mrs. Bethany L., sixth-grade teacher

Blessed Be...

Now to him who is able to do immeasurably more than all we ask or imagine, according to his power that is at work within us, to him be glory in the church and in Christ Jesus throughout all generations, for ever and ever!

Ephesians 3:20-21, NIV

~

Ten years ago on December eighth, my wife gave birth to a stillborn son. It was easily the most terrible day of my life. Every moment, from the time he was born to the time we crawled into bed that night, was a complete whirlwind. Yet, I remember it like it was yesterday.

It was just before Kaleb was born that I began hearing the song "Blessed Be the Name of the Lord"on the radio.[9] I immediately loved the song. The lyrics were stirring, and the melody was invigorating. It said everything my heart longed to say to the Lord – way better than I could have ever said it!

I began to sing the song from a brand new place. I had never before been in a desert. I had never before known a road marked with suffering. Could I bless His name in this desert? Could I really praise Him in the midst of this darkness?

He knows what is best.

I have many memories from that day and the days that followed— holding my son, helplessly looking into my wife's eyes, and making awkwardly painful phone calls to family and friends. The memory that stands out most is going to bed that night —there we were lying in bed, completely drained— when my wife and I began to pray.

I have learned through all of this that the Lord's leadership in my life is good. He knows what is best – and He gives far more than He takes away! Since Kaleb's death, the Lord has graciously given us Elise, Addison, Makayla, and a son, Kade. My heart sings, blessed be His glorious name.

God, Thank You for all You give us, and thank You for the things You take away. Give us the grace we need to bless Your name through the good times and the bad, for this is our heart's desire. Amen.

~ Mr. Welch, third grade

Always Watching

And you yourself must be an example to them by doing good works of every kind.
Let everything you do reflect the integrity and seriousness of your teaching.

Titus 2:7, ESV

~

My best friend in high school was class president, student director of the school play, and cheerleading captain. We all admired her for being a trustworthy leader even more than for her many accomplishments. After cheer practice one day, we walked to the parking lot discussing how best to deal with some conflicts that the girls on the junior high squad were having. I don't remember the details of our conversation, but I do recall a powerful statement she made to me that day: "Remember, they're always watching you." She was driving home the importance of modeling the values we wanted them to learn. Her words have echoed countless times in my memory. I heard them when I moved into my dorm room at a secular university, when I took a summer job as a nanny, when I ate lunch with my library co-workers, and when I started teaching.

Minds carefully weigh what we have taught them.

It is crystal clear to adults that small children imitate us. We adjust our behavior and language accordingly (who hasn't heard in a small, disapproving voice, "But we're not su-pposed to say the word stupid"?). Even when they grow older and more independent, we cannot underestimate the influence we still have over our children. They have not stopped watching. They notice the way we treat people who annoy us, what we say when we get angry, and how we handle stress. Their developing minds carefully weigh what we have taught them against what they see in us. My life is constantly being watched and weighed by others. Does it point to the love and grace of Christ or to my own selfishness and brokenness?

God, I recognize that I am incapable of living with love and integrity at all times. I rely on Your grace alone to redeem my mistakes. I know that You are watching my every move not because You are waiting for me to mess up, but because You love me as much as I love my own children.

~ A. Gillespie, secondary English

Setting Boundaries

And He said to them, "How is it that you sought Me?
Knew you not that I must be about My Father's business?"

Luke 2:49, KJV

~

Jesus had gone to Jerusalem with his parents and some of their friends to celebrate the feast of the Passover. He was twelve years old. The group of pilgrims began their return trip; but after one day, Mary and Joseph realized that Jesus was missing. They returned to Jerusalem and, three days later, found Jesus in the temple. He was sitting with the teachers, both listening and asking questions.

Use your experience and God's help to set meaningful boundaries.

WOW! Could you imagine the utter panic you would be experiencing if you could not locate your son or daughter for three days? Hopefully you would begin by praying. "Father, please protect our son. Keep him safe. Lead us to him, and let us feel Your peace."

Then you would call for assistance…police, friends, the media, anyone who might be willing to help. "God, please keep our son safe. Please lead us to him."

And then, hopefully, your prayers are answered; your son is found safe.

Hypothetical? NO! This situation will play out in some form during your lifetime. You will not always know where your son is. He might go off to college. He may take a job somewhere far away, maybe even out of the country. He will marry and have his own family, and you will not always know what is happening in their lives.

You must begin preparing for this while he is still young. Use your experience and God's help to set meaningful boundaries to protect him, but begin giving him little pieces of freedom. Let him make little decisions and then see and live with the consequences. Teach him how to be independent, making godly decisions on a small scale now; so that when he is ready to leave you to do his Heavenly Father's work, he has been properly prepared.

"Father, We thank You for parenting us. Thank You for showing us how to parent our children. Please help us to be good and godly parents. We pray in Jesus' precious name. Amen.

~ Bob Schluben, math

I See

We then, as workers together with him, beseech you also that ye receive not the grace of God in vain.

II Corinthians 6:1, KJV

~

God saved us for a reason. He saved us to minister to others. As a born again Christian, I have fully accepted the grace of God and eternal salvation. I certainly do not want to accept that eternal gift and not do something with it. I want to help others.

When I see the faces of my students, I see hope.

I look to the Apostle Paul and how he served others. By today's worldly standards, the Apostle Paul would have been considered a failure. He did not have a car, big house, money, or material possessions. Paul did not have the things that a large portion of society values today, and he did not seek them.

Paul left the world behind and answered God's call. Paul was only concerned with serving the Lord. Paul's rewards were not money, prestige, or material things. Paul's rewards were the people that he ministered to and won to Christ.

When I see the faces of my students who are sitting in my classroom, I see hope, I see beauty, and I see God's love. I am eternally grateful to the Lord for calling me into Christian education. I left behind the worldly things of no eternal value and exchanged them for students with souls that impact eternity.

Dear Lord, Let us always put You first in all things, including educating our children. Let us walk in Your light each and every day, teaching at home and at school, as You would have us teach for Your glory. Amen.

~ **Matt Shelton, secondary mathematics teacher**

Juggling Act

Come to me, all you who are weary and burdened, and I will give you rest.

Matthew 11: 28, NIV

~

I like to look like I have "it" together. I try to send out the vibe and create the appearance that I am a master juggler. Recently, one of our wonderful school moms popped into the library to see how I was doing and to let me know that she would be unable to volunteer because of a revision to her family's schedule that included her being there more for her family and less for the demands of others.

As I applauded her conviction to reprioritize, she shared with me a juggling illustration. She mentioned that we have many balls we try to juggle in life, some made of glass and others made of rubber. Our relationship with the Lord and our family members are the glass, and everything else is rubber. When we juggle so many balls, one is bound to drop. The glass balls will break, and the rubber balls will bounce back or away.

Often, when I am performing my juggling act, the most important relationships in my life suffer. I fail to make much time to be in the Word and congratulate myself on my five minutes of Bible reading. I rush, rush, rush, and justify lack of family dinners and game nights with the accomplishment of one more favor for one more person. During those times, I am so tired; and in all I try to accomplish, I still feel like I am failing. That is because I am failing, failing to be yoked with my Lord and Savior, Jesus Christ. Five minutes of Bible just to mark it off my task list is not enough. In a desperation to please, it is easy to become unbalanced and begin dropping balls, watching as some bounce and precious others break. Fortunately, the Lord uses the body of believers to encourage each other and the Holy Spirit to convict of needed change.

The Lord uses the body of believers to encourage each other.

When we are yoked with Him, the "rest" of life seems to fall into place. When we align our priorities in a God-pleasing fashion, life does not feel like a juggling act, and all that is precious to us stays intact. We will look like we have "it" together because we are united with the One Who is in control of the universe.

Heavenly Father, I confess to You the need to be in control of my life and to create an appearance of put togetherness. I praise You for the mercy and forgiveness You show me every time I mess up. I thank You for my family and the body of believers You have surrounded me with. Lord, I pray for time to build the relationship I have with You. Amen.

~ Alethea Beasley, communication arts

Making Mistakes

After the festival was over, while his parents were returning home, the boy Jesus stayed behind in Jerusalem, but they were unaware of it. Thinking he was in their company, they traveled on for a day. Then they began looking for him among their relatives and friends. When they did not find him, they went back to Jerusalem to look for him. After three days they found him in the temple courts, sitting among the teachers, listening to them and asking them questions. Everyone who heard him was amazed at his understanding and his answers. When his parents saw him, they were astonished. His mother said to him, "Son, why have you treated us like this? Your father and I have been anxiously searching for you."

Luke 2:43-48, NIV

~

Let them [our children] know we are not perfect.

One of the most fascinating figures in the New Testament is Joseph, husband of Mary. He learns to trust God despite what others must have been saying about his soon-to-be wife. Not only does he trust God, but he puts his full faith in Mary. As the father of Jesus, it must have often been challenging for Joseph, yet we never hear much about these challenges beyond when he and Mary could not find Jesus for three days!

Imagine the panic we feel when our young people slip out of our sight for a moment and think of how mad/glad/frustrated/relieved/angry/cranky/annoyed/ and overjoyed both Mary and Joseph must have felt when they found their boy in the temple. Even when you are the parents of the Son of God, there must have been times when it seemed too much.

We have all made mistakes, said things we wish we could swallow back into our mouths and minds. One of the most powerful things we can do for our children is to let them know we do make mistakes. When we do harm with words or actions, asking forgiveness and apologizing for our errors can be even more important than always being right. It is by showing our children how to admit an error, ask for forgiveness, and receive forgiveness that they will learn humility and begin to recognize that everyone makes mistakes. When we can admit our own errors and ask for forgiveness, we can lead our children to understand how Jesus is able to forgive us.

Dear God, Let me be honest with my children about the errors that I make. Let me be able to show them how to apologize with humility. Let me be an example of how to accept another's forgiveness. Let me, in turn, forgive my children when they come to me with mistakes. Let me know the humility of forgiving, even when the cost seems profound. Help me, Lord, to remember that no one is perfect, except You.

~ Anne Mussatti, communication arts

Creative Parenting

Put on your new nature, and be renewed
as you learn to know your Creator
and become like Him.
Colossians 3:10, NLT

Story Time

Jesus spoke all these things to the crowd in parables; He did not say anything to them without using a parable. So was fulfilled what was spoken through the prophet.

Matthew 13:34-35, NIV

~

Stories. We read them to small children, and then they read them to us. Eventually, they write their own stories, dissect stories in textbooks, and then read "the important stories" when they are in high school. Though I agree that Hamlet is deeper than, say, Eloise, I freely admit that both captured my imagination, and in the process, revealed something sinister about the human condition.

Truth can come from unlikely sources.

Jesus was big on stories, too. Parables or true-life tales-- do you notice He rarely differentiated between the two? Sure, modern scholars are quick to whip out their shiny lie detector, whose needle travels between extremes labeled true and false, or at least reality and fiction. But Jesus defies our static definitions and chooses instead to label His stories truth.

These stories are not equations. And I do not think they are a blueprint for life. I like to think of stories as vehicles of truth, because of the variety it conjures up: a shiny red Ferrari of truth, a rusted jalopy of truth, a reliable Toyota of truth. Truth is not delivered the same way every time; and as our children age, they will come to grips with the reality that truth can come from unlikely sources...like Hamlet, and Eloise, and surprise, surprise, the stories of life experiences of their parents and teachers.

Lord, Thank You for sharing so many stories with us in Your Word. Please help me to share stories of truth with my children, and to point out Your truth all around me.

~ Emily Stam, mom, theatre teacher and director

Look Deeper

The heavens declare the glory of God; the skies proclaim the work of His hands.

Psalm 19:1, KJV

~

Key to making someone a better artist is his or her learning how to see. It is important to really observe all of God's creation closely. You must take time to observe the visual details, looking further to see the complexities of how things really are. Often times, we rely on what we think we know, based on the masses of information and surface visual symbols observed over time. Learning to examine each thing as it really is in that moment is what allows an artist to capture more realistic representations.

In our busy lives, it is so easy to pass through the world on autopilot, not slowing down to absorb and appreciate the visual details in everything around us. Even with great technical ability in executing and rendering, sometimes even the most talented artists may get completely blocked with what to do next or how to see. Learning to see the empty space of the background or the nameless shapes in the shadows, bypassing the recognized symbols previously stored allows them to convey things as they really are when rendering realistic interpretation. This allows not only true appreciation of the level of detail in God's creation, but also creates an awareness of the need to look at all things deeper. In turn, we appreciate the beauty around us and, hopefully, glean a better understanding of the nature of God, developing a reverence for the Creator. The process of observing God's creation and creating enables us to connect more deeply with the Lord.

> Creating enables us to connect more deeply.

Lord, Thank You for giving us the ability to observe the details and beauty of Your creation. Help me to slow down and look closer at the seemingly ordinary things that can so easily be taken for granted. Help my child and me to connect on a deeper level with You through the process of observation.

~ Jana Jurkovich, art teacher

Weekly POW!

Praise the Lord, my soul. Lord my God, You are very great;
You are clothed with splendor and majesty.

Psalm 104:1, NIV

~

My husband Carey and I have been married for nearly forty years. We have four children, three of whom are now married. We have a high school teenager still in the home. Our seven grandchildren are the delight of our lives. I mention all of this to say I am overwhelmed by these undeserved blessings from the Lord. It is only by His grace and mercy!

I am overwhelmed by these undeserved blessings.

A few years ago, Carey asked me to connect with our children through the media that was most popular at that time and very new to us--email. His idea was to start emailing a "Psalm of the Week." He would choose the Psalm through his time with the Lord and then communicate it to me. I would then email the Psalm to our children. Then through subsequent conversations, we would talk about what the Psalm meant, or how God used it to bless our lives.

Of course, we would also have fun with it at times. Every family has to have a "jokester," and ours is not the exception! Our son, Marcellus, would many times find a humorous point in the Psalm and later "reply to all" his thoughts. We all get a good laugh through this as well.

In our day of acronyms (i.e., LOL, BRB, etc.), I now send out the emails with the subject "POW" (Psalm of the Week)!

Heavenly Father, In our sometimes "disconnected" world, help us to stay connected with those closest to our hearts. Help us find creative ways to stay close to You and to each other. In Jesus' name, Amen.

~ **Educating momma**

Experiencing Consequences

A prudent person foresees danger and takes precautions. The simpleton goes blindly on and suffers the consequences.

Proverbs 27:12, NLT

~

One of my favorite books as a child was *Mrs. Piggle-Wiggle.*[10] Mrs. Piggle-Wiggle was the neighborhood counsel when it came to raising naughty children; and her methods, though unconventional, always worked.

My favorite chapter was entitled "The Radish Cure." The main character was frustrated about being made to take a bath. Whenever his parents asked him to get in the shower, he bucked the system. Mrs. Piggle-Wiggle's answer was to give him the "reins" and allow the dirt to build up. Once it reached a certain thickness, she gave his parents special radish seeds to plant up and down his arms and legs. One bright morning, he was surprised to have plants growing out of him. They had itchy roots and tickly leaves! The poor character learned his lesson as the pain of plucking the radishes sent him happily to the bathtub for a good scrubbing. Self-cleansing was no longer an issue.

Teaching obedience is a tricky proposition. We want our children to obey us as their authority, without question or complaint. Yet, as they mature and their circle of authority grows, we must also equip them to consider the morality and logic of the commands. Wise parents sometimes allow their children to choose wrong and experience the pain that comes from poor choices.

> **Real consequence can be an amazing teacher.**

Allowing consequences may result in things such as tests with an "F"; outfits bringing public ridicule; their earned money wasted. However, to learn such lessons as a child will prevent much more devastating consequences as an adult. We are not with them "parenting" forever, nor would we want to be. Life lessons of real consequence can be an amazing teacher.

Dearest Lord Jesus, I do not like the idea of my children experiencing any consequences; I would much rather they were perfect! HA! I know You feel that way about me, too. So, right now, Lord, I am asking You to help me know when to cushion their fall and when to let them hit the ground. My desire is that all of my parenting and "Principaling" will bring them closer to knowing who You are. Thank You for loving and disciplining me, too. We are in this together, Lord! Amen.

~ Mrs. Gill, elementary principal

Leaving Classrooms

Never be lacking in zeal, but keep your spiritual fervor serving the Lord.

Romans 12:11, NIV

~

After spending ten years in the classroom and seven years as a pastor, I have learned a few important things. First, it is hard for people to listen to things they do not feel they need to know; and second, people learn better through experience. These truths are why science classrooms have labs, art classes have projects, and shop classes actually work with saws and machinery.

Faith and service need to be evident outside the church.

I am sure that you have realized the same thing that I have. Teaching the Bible and its call for service to the Lord take far more work than students simply sitting in a church or in a class. I can teach about service, love, and patience; but it falls on deaf ears if students have never truly had the chance to experience offering service, love, and patience.

Students have amazed me. I have watched them pray with homeless people at 2 A.M. in other countries. I have watched them tirelessly attempt to help inner city children learn theatre skills. I have watched them clean up after tornadoes devastated parts of Alabama.

Yes, young people learn in the classroom, but they grow when they serve others. What happens when they leave the classroom is far more important than what takes place inside. This fact is true for us as adults, as well. Our faith and service need to be evident outside the church even more so than on the inside.

Dear Lord, Help us to learn that life is far more than the sum of the knowledge we have obtained. Help us to love and serve, as that is how we will truly live.

~ **Wayne Stam, Bible teacher and future daddy**

Seeing Beauty

"Finally, brothers, whatever is true, whatever is honorable, whatever is just, whatever is pure, whatever is lovely, whatever is commendable, if there is any excellence, if there is anything worthy of praise, think about these things."

Philippians 4:8, RSV

~

Every teacher has an angle, and mine is beauty. I know very well that most of the images and sounds that barrage my sweet students are not beautiful. In this age of immediate access, there is little to encourage my students to prefer what is good, excellent and pure. Much in the cacophony of instant information seeks to destroy by making them insipid, bored, and blind to the beauty unfolding around them. I often think that if I could spend myself helping them gain a palate for what is true and beautiful, I would have spent myself well.

I find that such appreciation starts most easily by talking together about beautiful things. Take the Mona Lisa, for example. I have yet to meet a seventh grader who has a natural love for the odd painting. However, after five minutes of looking at the painting and simply describing it together, I have seen many, many students develop a deep appreciation for the piece of art. It is a strange transformation: apathy towards the painting turns to complete fascination. (When I told one class that a man stole the painting a century ago, several students insisted he deserved the death penalty!) Beauty possesses a transformative power that plays out in community without fail.

> Gain a palate for what is true and beautiful.

Visual art is not where we stop in exploring beauty. We see it in lives lived sacrificially in the face of danger during the Holocaust. We see beauty in a mind alive to the patterns around it in the life of Sir Isaac Newton. We see it in William Wilberforce's unceasing efforts to end the slave trade. We hear it in Bach's cello music. We see beauty especially in the gospel's rescuing us when every other faith in the world condemns us. Such talks are most fruitful when discussing together the person of Christ. Every little beauty is pointing to the ultimate beauty in Christ's redeeming the world.

Magnificent Father, The world is a spectacle of Your beautiful holiness and splendor. Oh, be gracious to give us eyes for Your grandeur! Teach us to appreciate beauty around us so that we are able to better see You. Your mercy is evident in that beauty exists at all. We do not deserve it, but You shower it upon us! Make us stewards of this world—transforming our conversations, our communities, our homes and our hearts into places of loveliness, purity, and goodness. We love You, and we thank You that we are a part of this story.

~ Middle school teacher

Seeking Everything

"In the beginning, God created the Heavens and the Earth.

Genesis 1:1, KJV

~

My father, a strong man of faith, was the NASA project chief who developed the complex computer program keeping the Apollo astronauts safe from the temperature extremes of space. A now-deceased family friend, Jim Irwin (the eighth man to walk on the moon) liked to describe how from the windows of the lunar module layers upon layers of galaxies can be seen resting upon what he called a multi-dimensional sheet of deep black velvet. Jim wondered how any person could see such wonders and not think of God.

Today we read about the brilliance of men who have devoted their lives to understanding quantum physics—"the Theory of Everything." Such intellectual giants labor to discover the origin of life and gravity, the meaning of black holes and dark matter, and whether we are part of a far larger multi-verse. Yet, brilliant as these people are, most struggle in vain because they do not begin from the profound quantum foundation easily discovered in Genesis.

My "prayer" is a poem I composed while pondering such things. It is my belief that the students who enter my classroom deserve nothing less than a teacher who will passionately pass on the baton of Truth to be found only in knowing the Creator of all.

The Mind Behind
By Greg Finch
Look through the silky velvet,
Scan past the scrolling skies of night,
Peer deep beyond the fabric,
Seek to know the Mind Behind!
The Mind Behind: Mystery!
The Mind Behind entangled webs.
The Quantum Mind Behind the physics.
The Mind Behind; the Life; the Breath.
The Mind Behind: The Substance.
The Mind Behind that dreams, invites.
The Mind Behind: The Light; The Meaning.
The Mind Behind; The Mind of Christ!
I'm striving for the Mind Behind.

~ Greg Finch, 20-year teacher and parent

More Teachable Moments

Rejoice always, pray continually, give thanks in all circumstances;
for this is God's will for you in Christ Jesus.

I Thessalonians 5:16-18, NIV

~

Often, as parents, we search for those opportunities that will be "teachable moments" for our children. We have such an intense desire for our children to mature into strong, compassionate, and godly men and women that we search for a momentous occasion in which we can stop our normal routine and "instruct" our children in the ways of God. We miss all the teachable moments that are woven throughout our regular day waiting for the "big one."

If we shift our perspective and look for those small moments within our daily lives in which we can teach our children about God's love and compassion, we will find that these little moments abound and can be an integral part of our everyday routines.

> **Teachable moments are woven throughout our regular day.**

As a mother of very young children, I found myself in the car a lot. At the time we lived in the country, so it was a long drive to the store. In order to keep my daughters cheerful en route, we would listen to children's music CDs. I became an expert on the lyrics to "Puff (The Magic Dragon)" and "Jelly Man Kelly." One song in particular remained embedded in our memories, and a family tradition emerged from this tune. Whenever we were in the car and we saw the moon, we would sing the sweet song, "I See the Moon" by James Merrill Brickman.[11] The lyrics talked about God blessing "somebody I want to see."

After singing the song, we would take turns stating whom it is each person wished they could see. We would then take a moment to pray for those individuals and ask for God's blessing on their lives. Now my girls are older, but we still sing the song and pray for our friends and family at the first sighting of the moon out our car window.

We should remember that the disciples learned as much, if not more, from Jesus by following Him around and watching Him live a life connected to His Heavenly Father as they did from listening to His Sermon on the Mount.

Dear Heavenly Father, Thank You for the gift of my children. Help me to model a life connected to You. Please reveal to me the teachable moments in our everyday routines.

~ **Junior high English teacher**

Team Player

As it is, there are many parts, but one body.

I Corinthians 12:2, NIV

~

Of course, parents have full authority over their own child. What often is not realized, however, is the fact that they are not supposed to have all of the answers. As each child is uniquely created with individual gifts and talents, there is no way any single person can guide, affirm, and counsel that child alone. Christ has called us to be a unified body, and raising a child is certainly one way He teaches us that we desperately need each other.

As Christians, we are supposed to reach out to one another.

At the end of her tenth grade year, my daughter looked at me and proclaimed, "I want to be an opera singer." My eyebrows went to my hairline. I knew little about opera and even less as to how to help someone become a dramatic mezzo soprano. That day a well-controlled panic set in. Over the years, I had heard several parents laughingly request "the manual" for child raising. In that moment, my spirit was yelling, "God, where is my manual for raising a godly opera singer?!"

Truth is that "the manual" would in reality be the world's largest encyclopedia set. We would have to switch volumes for every year, every phase, every changing friendship, and each life goal that is different than our own! I have since learned that the response to the manual request must be to diligently pray and to find the voices of wise counsel which surround every family.

As parents we are the primary educators; but, thankfully, alongside us are teachers, pastors, principals, dear friends, grandparents, and even opera singers—the list goes on. As Christians, we are supposed to reach out to one another for help and counsel. We are meant to reveal our vulnerabilities and need each other.

Be creative, persistent, and intentional in building the team called to bless your child. That way when those trials and opera songs come, you have wise counsel which supports your discernment of His perfect will.

Heavenly Father, my children are Yours. Help me wisely access the body of Christ in guiding them as they hone their gifts and talents for You.

~ Kimberlee Gill, academic dean

Encouraging Creativity

*One thing I ask from the LORD, this only do I seek: that I may dwell
in the house of the Lord all the days of my life, to gaze on the beauty
of the LORD and to seek him in his temple.*

Psalm 27:4, NIV

~

Some of my favorite memories for each of my children, so far, are not accomplishments they have made academically, or in the sports arena. They are not birthday parties or family outings. Yes, all those memories are good too, but my favorite ones, the ones that make my heart feel warm and tingly, are the times I remember them completely enveloped in the creative process.

God was very elaborate in creating.

When my oldest daughter was in first grade, we were learning about the states. She decided that she wanted to make a watercolor painting of state birds as we learned them. I have never been a bird-watching type of person, but seeing them through her seven-year-old eyes, I realized how beautiful they really are. This creating was a messy process and took time out of my homeschool day to set up and clean up, but the result at the end was worth it. We now have a bound photo book of her paintings to remind us that our God was very elaborate in creating these little creatures. How much more did He invest in us?

Creativity in my youngest child looks a little bit different. She wears her creativity like a canvas every day. She likes to wear as many layers as possible, expressing her love for color, shapes, and the busyness of patterns and textures. She finds joy in the "different," and likes to surround herself with "beauty." I think God does this with us, too. He created us in His image, and likes to be surrounded by us in our creative beauty.

How do you encourage creativity in your child? Turn off the electronics, do not require them to color inside the lines, let them experiment, let them fail, and encourage the process, not the product. In those moments you will rejoice to see a reflection of our Creator in them.

Father God, Thank You for all the beauty that You have created around us. Thank You for Your gift of creativity that lives in each of us. Help us to put aside our busyness to let our children access this gift. Thank You for the journey. Amen.

~ Trish Teilborg, early elementary teache

Creative Exploration

Oh Lord, how manifold are your works! In wisdom have you made them all.

Psalm 104:24a, ESV

~

God is a magnificent artist.

I have fond memories of camping as a young child. Each summer we would travel to faraway places. I never minded sleeping in a tent or eating camp food. I looked forward to the excitement of the trip and to being surrounded by nature.

My dad would spend hours packing the car, and then we would drive together to a new destination. It was in the days before technologies like GPS, cell phones, and car DVD players. Instead, we used maps to find our way and spent hours listening to old country music and to books on tape.

By the time I was ten years old, I had been to over half of the continental United States. It was exciting to return to school in the fall and share my travel stories with my teachers. I always felt proud that I had gone somewhere during the summer break.

My dad would strap our bikes to the back of the car and we would ride all over the campsites exploring. Sometimes my sister and I would meet friends from other places, and we would spend the day together. We would hike, swim, rent boats, go canoeing, and visit historical monuments. We also used to bring our dolls and set up a campsite for them on the picnic table. In the evening my dad would often play his guitar, and we would sing around the fire while we roasted hot dogs and marshmallows.

As an adult I now realize how challenging and expensive it can be to plan summer vacations of any kind. I am very grateful that my dad made sacrifices to make these trips possible for our family.

Plan a trip for your family. Explore the world, making memories that will last a lifetime. God is a magnificent artist, and His majesty can be seen throughout the beauty of His creation.

Lord, Please help me to remember how important it is to take time to explore the world that You created. Please protect my family and lead me to opportunities where I may spend time outside enjoying Your amazing creation. Please remind me often that Your desire is that I put my family first. Please continue to protect the time our family spends together. Thank You for always watching over us. Amen.

~ Sra. Briseno, mommy and Spanish teacher

Unique Creation

So God created man in his own image, in the image of God he created him; male and female he created them.

Genesis 1:27, KJV

~

Many times, I have been so impressed with something a student, irrespective of age, has created. The statement that best captures what I feel is, "I love the way you see the world!"

We are all surrounded by the beauty of God's creation; it is a constant source of the ultimate inspiration. Each person has been uniquely created by God to interpret images in a unique way through the process of creating. It may be how someone chooses to zoom in and frame a portion of a still life that makes his art look completely different. Perhaps it is an unusual color combination that evokes a certain mood or feeling. In the act of creation, the individuality of each person truly comes to light. As each person is unique, so unique is his creation.

> Have a specific plan, purpose and way of seeing the world.

God has created us in His image, including the longing and ability to create. When we are composing or arranging, whether visual elements, words, or music, we are creating. The process of creating makes us very close to that aspect of God. We have a specific plan, purpose and way of seeing the world and communicating it to others.

God created us with the ability to express ourselves visually. Though you may not be trained in the arts, your God has provided a world to inspire you and your child. Rejoice in being surrounded by the beauty and variety of God's creation. Within it we cannot help but be inspired to create!

Lord, Help me to see my child as Your unique creation. Help me appreciate the way that my child sees the world and his ability to leave a mark that is as unique as You have made him. Help me to encourage my child to create and try new things. Help my child understand his value and ability to share his unique voice and interpretation with the world.

~ Jana Jurkovich, art teacher

Life Story

I urge you to live a life worthy of the calling you have received.

Ephesians 4:1, NIV

~

We are all writing a story with our lives, each and every day as we live it. The children around us are writing the beginning of their life story. The events they survive and people they encounter will affect that story. The adventures, the friendships, those first encounters with God—they will shape and form these children before us into adults.

Trust God with our dreams for our children.

As a writer, I know that nobody likes a story with a passive protagonist. No, the exciting tales are ones where the main character goes after what he wants and struggles to obtain it. A pet dragon, survival in a strange land, the lost treasure—what is it that we strive for? Are our children being passive protagonists, merely reacting to the events in their lives? Or are they being active participants in their story, searching the heart of God to find what He wants, and making that their number one goal?

And as adults, are we open to the adventures God has for us, regardless of their effect on our status or financial security? Do we trust God with our dreams for our children?

May we all know the thrill of living a full life story as a protagonist who is chasing after God and serving His children—a life worthy of our calling.

Thank You, Father, for my child's life story and the events that have led her to this day. Please give me grace on those days when my child's story has conflict, and mercy on those days when my child sees me as his evil antagonist. Help my family to live the life You have for us and to embrace Your adventures at every turn.

~ Emily Stam, future mommy, theatre teacher and director

Ideas Available

For the Lord gives wisdom, from His mouth come knowledge and understanding.

Proverbs 2:6, ESV

~

Required reading of *The Scarlet Letter* by Nathaniel Hawthorne is pretty typical for high school. As an English teacher, it was always difficult to pull students through this amazing, but complex novel. Year after year, I would impose note taking and pop quizzes to ensure the reading was actually occurring. One year, I had a particularly difficult class.

God... Help me to remember to ask You first.

Teachers know that entire classes have personalities. This group was incredibly creative, full of musicians and artists. They were funny! I constantly had to smother back laughter and re-direct them. They most definitely did not prioritize academics. Therefore, reading about an embroidering pilgrim lady in an archaic society had zero appeal. I pulled every trick I knew as a teacher to be exciting, interesting, and downright authoritarian. Nothing worked. We were supposedly through chapter three, and only a brave few had cracked the book. Finally, I asked my Lord full of wisdom, "God, what can I do to get these kids into this story?" (Side note: I am getting better at asking him FIRST rather than when all else fails!)

My prayer was said in the car on the way home from school after a particularly draining class period. The Lord answered loud and clear, "Have them embroider letter A's while you read the book to them." I began arguing with the Lord (not smart). "God, I don't have embroidery hoops, needles or thread. That will not work." He guided my eyes to look up, and there on road in front of me was a fabric store. I sighed and pulled into the parking lot. I walked in and asked for a manager and explained my educational plight and "my" idea for embroidering with my class. Long story short: she immediately *donated* everything I needed: twenty-four hoops, linen cloth, and red and golden thread. She threw in a red fabric paint pen, just in case.

The next day I demonstrated the satin stitch, the daisy stitch, and the chain stitch. The students got excited. I was in shock. Off they went designing their scarlet letter A's. I began reading the novel aloud while they stitched their designs. They offered comments on the personality of Hester Prynne. "She must have been so creative; how could she handle being in bondage to the laws?" "She must have been patient." Yep. God knew.

Amazing. God, of course, You understand how to inspire Your kids. God, inspire me through the power of artistry; and please, help me remember to ask You first!

~ Kimberlee Gill, former English teacher

Embrace Unexpected

Therefore, if anyone is in Christ, he is a new creation;
the old has passed away, the new has come.

II Corinthians 5:17, RSV

~

While it is great to have a plan and vision for creating, and for life in general, sometimes it is the unexpected that can take things in a new direction, yielding even better results. Our plans are often less creative, more routine, and in line with how we usually think. Thinking outside of the box may not always come as naturally. Learning to embrace the unanticipated, adjust and take on a new, possibly even better direction is important.

In life, the unexpected will happen.

An accidental puddle of permanent ink dropped randomly on a drawing where every stroke had been painstakingly applied to render a perfect representation of what was intended forces the artist to take the creation in an entirely new direction. The first response may be to simply abandon the work completely, as it may seem to be "ruined" in light of the original intention. However, the response to the unexpected and thinking of other solutions can create so much more than ever intended. The ink blob could be transformed into something that looks intentional, which can add additional interest to the composition. The background may be cut away to remove the blob entirely, and mount the creation on a contrasting background that adds interest in the negative space. Additional media may be layered over to conceal the blob, adding depth or texture.

In life, the unexpected will happen. Our response to those events can either bring an attitude of defeat or resilience. Learning to see the opportunities in the unexpected and realizing that sometimes things can be even better as a result is an important life lesson to pass on to our children. Regardless, much is learned in the journey of adapting.

Lord, When things do not go as I had hoped, help me to see new opportunities and persevere. Thank You for not viewing us as permanently broken, but to give us the opportunity to become new and better creations through You. Help me to pass this on to my child.

~ Jana Jurkovich, art teacher

Encouraging Dreamers

Whatever you do, work at it with all your heart,
as working for the Lord, not for human masters.

Colossians 3:23, NIV

~

We all dream…usually at night, and sometimes during meetings or class. We all have things that we want to accomplish and try, and we all probably have had someone help us accomplish our goals.

When I was a little girl, I wanted to be an artist when I grew up. I thought it would be the coolest job! I spent my allowance on a sketchbook and some pastels and started to draw, sketch, and paint everything I saw. My parents were very supportive of my dream and even enrolled me in an art class over the summer. Boy, was I excited! The class was just for kids, but in an art studio, so it seemed really important. Yet, after my first class was over, I was not as excited about art. I kept going to the classes, but my perceived ability was decreasing with every class. Looking back, I am clear on two truths: (1) I little artistic talent, and (2) My parents encouraged me anyway. They sacrificed their time and money to affirm my dreams and allow me to figure things out. Even now, I am humbled.

> God allows our dreams and goals to change as He molds us.

We must encourage our children to dream. God has given each of them a specific talent and desire. Encourage them to try different things and find their own gifting empowers their worth and an understanding of whom they are in Christ.

Though it may seem a waste of time and money, we must allow them to pursue their dreams. Giving the time and resources will allow them to reach their God-given potential. We should encourage and motivate them to work on their dream with all their might, "as working for the Lord." Over time, God will allow their dreams and goals to change as He molds them into the person He created them to be for His glory.

Dear God, Thank You for creating us with dreams. Give us chances to pursue our dreams as we work for You. Allow our kids to dream big dreams and follow them knowing that they have parents who support them and a God Who knows what is best. Amen.

~ Miss Schmidt, early elementary

Creative Thinking

See, I will create new heavens and a new earth. The former things
will not be remembered, nor will they come to mind.

Isaiah 65:17, NIV

~

In my previous job, I worked with adults in the business world, facilitating teams to evaluate processes and solve problems. The need for creative thinking skills was daily brought to light. However, it often seemed difficult for adults to tap into these skills after a lifetime of being conditioned to think like everyone else.

The creative process adds such value to our families.

One of my desires as an art teacher is to help students admire and preserve the creative process. The skills of creativity are valuable, not just for the sake of creating for pleasure, but for all facets of life. The creative process adds such value to our families, our hobbies, and even our workplace, regardless of the type of work. Providing opportunities to imagine, explore and reflect will develop skills that will be beneficial throughout life in many future endeavors. Examining and building things and the subsequent problem solving that results through the process can provide valuable lessons.

Operating in creativity also brings the body of Christ together! While there is opportunity for growth in individual pursuits, there are many ways in which collaborative, creative exploration can also expand ideas. Capitalizing on opportunities to create with your child can be a way to bond more tightly. Creative moments enable us to learn together and see each other and the world in new ways.

Expand into all that is possible and create!

Lord, How blessed we are to have the ability to think creatively like You, the Creator.
Help me pause, reflect and think in new ways. Help me look for opportunities for my
child that will stimulate the creative thinking that You have instilled in us all.

~ **Jana Jurkovich, secondary art**

For Gary

But even if I am being poured out like a drink offering on the sacrifice and service coming from our faith, I am glad and rejoice with all of you.

Philippians 2:17, NIV

~

I started off a teacher,
Clear back in second grade.

Mrs. Murray gave me Gary,
A co-student who had strayed.

Gary couldn't read well,
And I read all the time.

It was a joy to read with him,
And I did not take a dime.

I soon found his house was different;
He had no help at home.

He spent his time just building things
While he was all alone.

His parents had to work a lot;
They couldn't help with school.

Somehow I grasped the circumstance
Was what made Gary seem a fool.

We began playing recess together,
And I quizzed the daily drill.

He made me little trinkets,
And I took them with a thrill.

I told my mom, "He's really smart.
Just different smart than school."

We wished there were an elementary
Where he could wield his tools.

Second grade was finished.
There was never shared class again.

I wondered what had happened to him
But life moves on from friends.

He did not graduate with me,
I'd heard that he'd flunked out.

I went off to college,
With scholarships in tout.

One college summer I read a paper,
And my heart began to moan.

A self-inflected death, his end.
My first student all alone.

We were eight in second grade,
I taught him with little skill.

But his life gave me inspiration;
It's carried with me still.

Each child is so gifted.
Each one a purposed call.

Each teacher has a mission
To embrace them one and all.

My eyes still weep for that sweet boy
As I relay my tale.

And my still promise to sweet Gary,
On my watch, they will not fail.

Jesus, help us see each other.

~ A teacher

Loving Parenting

*Dear children, let us not love with words or
speech but with actions and in truth.*
I John 3:13, NIV

God's Favorite

As the Father has loved me, so have I loved you. Now remain in my love.

John 15: 9, NIV

~

I have had many different kinds of students walk through my door bringing labels from their past: bright students, challenged students, "good" students, "bad" students, spiritually rich students, and spiritually bankrupt students. Each one had specific needs that required my attention; some more than others. Most certainly, all had the need to know I loved them.

He fully loves you right where you are.

I paint in the summer. I enjoy it because every day I can see what I have done. I can step back from a house and know what has been accomplished. Teaching is much different. I often spend my summers wondering if I made a difference, thinking about what I could have done differently, or better. Did my class receive what they needed? Did they know I loved them and cared about them?

Everyone needs to know that God cares for him or her. It is our deepest need. Thank God for His love. The essence of God's being is wholehearted love. From eternity past, the three persons in the Trinity have loved each other with all of their heart. This is how the Father loves the Son, and the Son loves the Spirit, …. The only way that God loves His family (the Trinity and the Church) is with all of His heart and in great humility. Truly, as a body of Christ, our job is to consistently and to purposefully reflect that love to one another.

The words Jesus spoke in John 15 seem unrealistic to our natural thinking, but just because we do not feel the power of this truth does not lessen its reality. Jesus has authority to teach of God's love, and His truth is the ultimate statement of our worth. Nothing we can do will ever earn us more love or cause God to love us any less. He fully loves you right where you are today. Bask in the glory of knowing that today, you are His favorite!

Father, Thank You for Your love for me. I pray that You would let me see and feel what You see and feel about me. I long to understand Your love better and overflow it to all those around me. Amen.

~ Mr. Welch, third grade

Perfect Love

Jesus Christ is the same yesterday and today and forever.

Hebrews 13:8, NIV

~

Being completely honest, I must admit that I am not a parent and am unsure at this point in my life what God's plan is for me regarding children. I have, however, worked with children for a number of years and hope, one day, I will be able to offer advice as a seasoned parent.

> God's love restores and replenishes.

Although I have not yet shared in the joys and trials of parenting, as an elementary art teacher and prior nanny to a dear family of four children (for five years), my eyes were opened to many of the ups and downs that make-up the roller coaster ride that parenting really is. Joyous occasions seem to be followed by occurrences of drama; moments of structure and organization almost always landslide into a pit of chaos and confusion.

The most challenging experience as an "almost" parent of four was having enough love to share with the precious children that I spent my days and nights with when mom and dad were not able to be around.

Of course, there were wonderful moments when I recited in my head, "My cup runneth over!"; moments of feeling so blessed by the hearts of these children that I thought that joy might explode right out of me.

However, there were also times when I found myself reciting, "Can't I get a break, God; Just one moment alone?" This "parenting" gig was overwhelming, to say the least. Some days I felt that I had no more sanity to hold on to. What is harder to admit is that I felt that there were moments when I felt that I had no more love to give.

Each time I returned to the pit of lovelessness, asking for God's help, I was reminded of His perfect love for us. God never asks, "Can't you give me a break? Won't you leave me alone for a few minutes?" What a perfect love: a love that never fails. It is never changing nor is it even the slightest bit intermittent.

God's love restores and replenishes the love that my human flesh cannot maintain.

Dear Lord, Thank You so much for the blessing it is to share each day with a child. Thank You for loving me in my good moments and even in my bad moments. Please remind me to love and treat others according to Your command: with selflessness, humility, and with joy.

~ Elementary art teacher

Pressing In

O God, you are my God; I earnestly search for you. My soul thirsts for you; my whole body longs for you in this parched and weary land where there is no water. I have seen you in your sanctuary and gazed upon your power and glory. Your unfailing love is better than life itself; how I praise you! I will praise you as long as I live, lifting up my hands to you in prayer. You satisfy me more than the richest feast. I will praise you with songs of joy. I lie awake thinking of you, meditating on you through the night. Because you are my helper, I sing for joy in the shadow of your wings. I cling to you; your strong right hand holds me securely.

Psalms 63: 1-8, NLT

~

I remember being in a church service years before having my twins and hearing a new worship song that touched my heart. The lyrics of the song by Kari Jobe entitled *The More I Seek You* say: "The more I seek you. The more I find you. The more I find you. The more I love you. I wanna sit at your feet, drink from the cup in your hand, lay back against you and breathe, feel your heartbeat. This love is so deep; it's more than I can stand. I melt in your peace, it's overwhelming."[13] This song captured me. It seemed to paint this perfect and serene picture of us leaning against God, relaxing in His perfect presence.

If we simply seek Him, we can bask at His feet.

It is as if God is this strong and powerful tree, lovingly providing shade and serenity. I did not quite grasp the emotion of this relationship until I had my children.

I remember, on several occasions, my son and daughter sitting at my feet, grasping so tightly that I would be walking around the room with a child on each leg. I remember my daughter, Emma, sitting on the floor by my feet and leaning against my legs. She looked up at me and smiled so sweetly. God immediately brought the lyrics of that worship song back to my mind. Although I am not perfect, my daughter wanted to be as close to me as possible. She is small in comparison to me, and grasped on to the part of me she could hold. Don't we feel small in comparison to God? I think we sometimes feel like we cannot reach Him. Yet, if we simply seek Him, we can bask at His feet, feeling comforted by our Heavenly Father the same way my daughter and son feel comforted by holding onto me. How He loves our finding complete rest in Him!

Jesus, Help me to sit at Your feet the same way my children enjoy and feel comforted sitting at mine. Wrap Your arms around me, God; for I can do nothing without You. I love You and thank You. In Jesus' name, Amen.

~ Jennie Schueller, fourth grade

Touching Lives

*Fulfill ye my joy, that ye be likeminded, having the same love,
being of one accord, of one mind. Let nothing be done through strife or vainglory;
but in lowliness of mind let each esteem other better than themselves.*

Philippians 2:2-3, KJV

~

Being a teacher has taught me many things. Students are entering my classroom with so many things going on in their lives. Some of them are dealing with divorce, death in the family, or a sick family member. Doing schoolwork is the last thing on their mind. The past few years it does seem like so many more kids are hurting. Unfortunately, it is so easy to get wrapped up in my own world and not notice what they are going through. It is my job to make the seven hours they are at school a little brighter. Sometimes they just need a smile as they enter the classroom or a note on their desk letting them know I am thinking of them. I know each year God puts the students I am supposed to have in my room. I pray that I will take time to notice when one of them needs encouragement.

Take the time to notice.

I encourage you to take the time to notice and care for the people around you. Letting people see that you care about them can go a long way. You never know whose life you can touch with just a simple smile.

Dear Jesus, I pray that I will be sensitive to others' needs, especially the needs of the students in my class. Thank You for being an example to me of how to love and care for others. Thank You for loving me. Amen.

~ Ashley Kates, fifth-grade teacher

Unconditional Love

The LORD is like a father to his children, tender and
compassionate to those who fear him.

Psalm 103:1, NLT

~

Like all children at some point, my son is going through a time of temper tantrums and meltdowns. It seems everything we tell him has a test that involves spouts of yelling and hitting. He will have these escalated moments followed by peaks of his normal calm behavior. From the example that I constantly show when I make a mistake with my children, he is learning to quickly and sincerely apologize after the fact. He still lacks impulse control, which is natural for a three-year-old child. Although I understand mentally that this stage of life is normal, I find it immensely difficult emotionally to deal with on a daily basis. It becomes exhausting.

There is no way to earn or lose His love.

Even though this has been a tough stage to get past with my son, I love him no less. I am still there to pick him up when he falls and kiss his hurts away. I still take care of his needs and try to give him the best I can, even on the toughest of days.

Isn't this exactly what God does for us? He loves us, pure and simple. There is no way to earn or lose His love. He simply loves us because we are His children. The closest we can come to understanding God's unconditional love is with our kids. They are a part of us, and we love them. Even in their worst moments, we still love them.

God showed me that just like I want the best for my son, He wants the best for me. When I have spiritual tantrums, He is constant and faithful in taking care of me. When we come to Him and ask for forgiveness, He chooses to forget our wrongs and give us chance after chance until we get it right. God, help me to have grace and unconditional love towards my children.

This is best displayed, of course, through our own humble examples. Let us try to emulate our Creator and show tenderness and compassion toward our children, giving them glimpses of God's eternal and unconditional love.

God, I come before You as Your child. Help me to receive Your unconditional love and give it out to those around me. Let me be quick to ask for forgiveness, quick to forget a wrong, and always willing to love the way You intended. Help me, as a mother, be an example for my children in grace and mercy. Let my example lead them to Your salvation. In Jesus' Name, Amen.

~ Jennie Schueller, fourth-grade teacher

Maskless Freedom

For there is nothing covered that will not be revealed, nor hidden that will not be known.

Luke 12: 2-3, NKJV

~

There is a certain freedom one feels when he is able to stand before his peers as he truly is without hiding behind a false image created to keep the world from seeing the real him. I had been hiding behind such a mask for years, and the glue that held that mask firmly in place was my pride. What would people think if they knew that I was not

The mask came unglued.

really happy or that my marriage was a disaster? I must show the world that I am a mature Christian who is spiritually strong, not a wounded animal limping through life. Unfortunately, my proud mask and daily routine kept me from receiving the help I desperately needed.

One day during faculty devotions, after a particularly difficult morning at home, the mask came unglued. I tried to hold back the tears, but it was no use. I had taken all I could take, and the floodgates opened. As I let the truth out between sobs, I felt an arm wrap around me, then another. Instead of the judgment I had feared, I was met with a well-spring of love, prayer, and encouragement.

My healing began that day. I received the help I needed to break away from a harmful situation. I am free from the darkness and deception—free to be who God called me to be and do the work God has called me to do.

God gives us fellow believers to help us overcome the battles we face. If we hide the truth from each other, we are not only hurting ourselves but the body of Christ.

I thank my Lord daily for the love that pours from Him through others to fill my thirsty soul.

Lord, Help us to truly become one body. Help us remove our masks and allow You to weave us together as a beautiful tapestry that reveals Your story of love and redemption.

~ An educator

Love Limitless

You have heard that it was said, 'Love your neighbor and hate your enemy.'
But I tell you, love your enemies and pray for those who persecute you,
that you may be children of your Father in heaven.

Matthew 5:43-45, NIV

~

Christ puts on loving limitless.

As human beings we find it easy to love those who love us and hate those who hate us. It is important to model to our young people the importance Christ puts on loving limitless that is, loving people, even if they are not easy to love. Children pick up on their parents' words and attitudes. If they hear them wishing ill on a coworker or family member, they think it is acceptable to wish ill on a bully, a friend who has betrayed them, or a frustrating teacher.

A more Christ-centered approach would be for the parents to express sorrow that someone has enough ill-will in their heart to act against them in such a way and to pray for those people with their spouse and children. This way the children see that love does not extend just to those who are nice to them, but it extends to all. This exercise of discretion and mercy leads to a deeper and more meaningful relationship with our Father in heaven.

Dear Heavenly Father, I pray for the parents of my students. Please help them to model mercy, prayer, and love for those who do them harm so that their children can grow up to be like You. Amen.

~ Math teacher

Forgiveness

And when you stand praying, if you hold anything against anyone,
forgive him, so that your Father in heaven may forgive you your sins.

Mark 11:25, NIV

~

Last Sunday our pastor spoke about forgiveness. He said if there is someone in your life or your past with whom you have had conversations in your mind, there is likely a lack of forgiveness. At first I just laughed it off as though I have never done that.

I choose to forgive.

But then I thought, "I do that!" I have conversations in my head with my father about all the times he has hurt me. I used to cry; then it turned to anger, and now? Now I just do not feel much at all. I thought that meant I had forgiven him. I do pray about it, and I ask God to help me forgive. However, when my mind is honest, I know that forgiveness is still in progress.

Forgiveness seems so simple. It is a choice. God forgave me; why can't I do the same? It seems silly to keep all that hurt, to let someone who has no idea what he has done have such an impact on my life. So, I choose to forgive him, thankful that the Christ in me is there to help the process along as I die daily to self. This death is not easy. It involves giving up the dreams of what should have been for a harsh reality. This forgiveness demands a release of grace.

Walk with me. If there is someone you need to forgive, pleases trust me when I say, they are not the ones dying inside. You are. For yourself and your children, embrace the gift of forgiveness.

Heavenly Father, Thank You for loving us and for sending Your Son to forgive our sins. Please help us to forgive those who have wronged us. Your Word says if we forgive others, You will also forgive us. We praise You for Your mercy and goodness. Amen.

~ Growing teacher

Forgiven, Forgive

Be kind to one another, tenderhearted, forgiving one another,
as God in Christ has forgiven you.

Ephesians 4:32, RSV

~

Forgiveness
(Song and lyrics)
By Matthew West

It's the hardest thing to
give away
And the last thing on
your mind today
It always goes to those
that don't deserve
It's the opposite of how
you feel
When the pain they
caused is just too real
It takes everything you
have just to say the
word...
Forgiveness[12]

This journey called life is fraught with brokenness—sickness, disease, poverty, tragic accidents, natural disasters, suffering of all kinds. And in the midst of these lies one of the most difficult to grapple with, the hurt and grief of fractured relationships. Relationships crying out for reconciliation, healing, and forgiveness.

"Just move on." "Just get over it." These are the lines that we hear others often glibly say after seeing the effects of a deep wound from another. Those deepest wounds are too often the wounds of a friend. David the King certainly agonized over this: "If an enemy were insulting me, I could endure it; if a foe were rising against me, I could hide. But it is you, a man like myself, my companion, my close friend, with whom I once enjoyed sweet fellowship at the house of God, as we walked about among the worshipers." (Psalm 55:12-14)

Forgiveness assumes that a genuine wrong has been committed. It does not minimize either the wrong or the painful results; rather, forgiveness says, "Though I was truly wronged, I will not allow that wrong to rule my life. Instead, I will release the wrong to the Lord, for He is the one Who brings true justice." Forgiveness, when matched with genuine repentance by an offender, can lead to reconciliation. Yet sometimes reconciliation is not possible in this life; nevertheless, when we forgive, we allow the Lord to touch our hearts and heal us more deeply. We take down the barriers between ourselves and others so that we might enjoy deeper and more loving relationships. We allow the grace of God so that we might live more fully as forgiven, whole people.

Lord, Heal my heart as I commit to forgive others as You have so graciously forgiven me. Teach me compassion for others in their hurts and sorrow that I might be a model of Your healing love and grace.

~ A long-time educator

Love First

Dear friends, since God so loved us, we also ought to love one another.

I John 4:11, NIV

~

On May 15, 1977, I made a vow before God in the sacred covenant of marriage. I promised to love, honor, and obey my groom, Carey Walden Casey.

> We are committed to each other for a lifetime.

Just weeks prior to this day, Carey and I prayed about this possibility. We were both students at UNC Chapel Hill—I a senior and Carey a junior. Carey played on the football team, so we had to eliminate many possible wedding dates due to conflicts with the football schedule. After searching diligently for the soonest possible date, we found if we did not get married within the next few weeks, we would need to wait another year. Neither of us liked that solution, as we were in love and believed in our hearts that God was leading us to this union.

You see, Carey and I spent quite a bit of time in prayer. We would go on prayer walks in Chapel Hill. There was a huge rock protruding out of the ground just off the beaten path through campus that we called our "prayer rock." We would stop there often to pray, asking for God's guidance. We asked for wisdom in planning not only a wedding, but a lifetime of ministry together. We specifically asked the Lord to make our marriage a witness, that He would use our marriage to be a blessing to others.

Now, I am not claiming a perfect marriage at all. But I am saying Carey and I are committed to each other for a lifetime. God has used our years together to bless and encourage other couples and families.

God is love, and we must always keep "Love First."

Heavenly Father, Thank You for first loving us. Thank You for the families You have given us. I ask for your blessings over us all, as we seek You daily. In Jesus' name, Amen.

~ Melanie Casey, second-grade teacher and joyous wife

Contagious Kindness

Be kind and compassionate to one another...

Ephesians 4:32a, NIV

~

They learned the power of pausing in the moment to reach out in kindness.

I recently heard a story about some construction workers who were working on a building adjacent to a children's hospital.

One day as they were working, they saw a little girl waving from her window in the hospital. The construction workers waved back, not thinking much about it. The next day they saw the same little girl in the same window holding a sign that read, "Hi. My name is Abby. What are your names?" The men quickly found a piece of paper and wrote their names. The next day they saw Abby sitting in her window saying, "I am seven years old. How old are you?" The construction workers replied. This simple sort of conversation went on for several days. One day Abby was not sitting in her window with a piece of paper to continue the conversation, so one of the men called the hospital. The man told the nurse that he was a construction worker across the street and about their interactions with Abby and that they had not seen her today. The nurse, very aware with the now famous conversation and knowing it was not protocol, told the man that Abby had taken a quick turn for the worse and had died that last night. The man got off the phone with the nurse and then ordered flowers for the family telling them who he was and what he and his friends had been doing. Several days later the family came to tell the construction workers thank you. They expressed their thanks and told the men that Abby told everyone about her construction worker friends and how they had brightened her last days.

I'm sure that those construction workers were never told how to act in a situation like this one. Yet somewhere, they learned the power of pausing in the moment to reach out in kindness. It is power that reaches far beyond the recipient. Their kindness affected the doctors, nurses, other patients, other construction workers, and now, you. Kindness is contagious and can spread quickly.

Being kind is not something you can teach with words. Every parent strives for their children to be kind, but if children do not see adults modeling kindness, the teaching will have no effect.

Jesus, Please give me opportunities to show Your love and kindness to others. Thank You for being the perfect example of how to be kind to others. I want to be more like You, but I need Your help. Amen.

~ Early elementary teacher

Fruit Squeezin'

Lo, children are an heritage of the Lord, and the fruit of the womb is his reward.

Psalms 127:3, KJV

~

My son was in eighth grade the day I looked at him across the room and realized my little boy seemed all grown up. I had a panic moment; I could not remember the last time that I held him and just breathed him in. I knew I should not do it, but I could not help myself. "Hey," I pleaded unconvincingly, "I need you to come sit on my lap." He looked at me like I was crazed, which, in that moment, I was. I shared with sad eyes that I could not remember the last time I had held him and I needed to mark that moment in my mind. He slow-grinned and came over to plop his giant body down. I was totally squished, but I wrapped my arms around his waist and held on tight. I got about fifteen seconds before he let me know my time was up and bounded out the door.

> Squeeze them [your children] all you can.

This devotion serves as a clarion call to all parents with young children. Love them deeply and squeeze them all you can. Stare into their eyes and listen to their stories, cherishing the sweet baby voice and the elementary school softness. Tell the tales of your family and share your testimony while they still want to take time to listen. Brag on your romance story with your spouse, sharing how your love created the best fruit ever--them.

As my children have grown to become successful, independent adults who love Jesus, I am proud to watch them fulfill the call on their lives. However, the mommy heart does, from time-to-time, miss the clutter, the chaos, and the sweet times spent rocking by the window. I am grateful to my Savior Who rewarded me with such sweet, sweet gifts.

Lord, Thank You for my sweet, all grown up babies. I know You adore them as much as I do. In their life trials, Holy Spirit, would You help them to remember they are loved beyond measure? Prompt my heart to know when they may need to hear once again that they will always be my greatest treasure.

~ Mama teacher

Thriving Families

Has not the one God made you? You belong to him in body and spirit.
And what does the one God seek? Godly offspring. So be on your guard,
and do not be unfaithful to the wife of your youth.

Malachi 2:15, NIV

~

One of the issues God exposed in Malachi was that the nation of Israel was not guarding their marriages, and this lack of care was causing marriages to fall short of His design. In Malachi 2:15, God is returning the Israelites to the purpose of marriage, helping them see that to preserve marriage, it must be guarded. As believers, this guardianship is an important message to embrace in our fallen culture. Then, as our marriages thrive, so thrive our children.

Protect the unity of your marriage.

Seek God's purpose for your marriage. God has put you together for a purpose. As a couple you should seek this purpose. In response to God's leading, my wife and I created a written mission statement for our marriage so we can know how to prioritize life issues. Additionally, it has given us God's reason behind our marriage's existence, helped illuminate the path to get out of difficult times, and provided purpose for our journey. Do you know God's purpose for your marriage?

Establish boundaries that protect the unity of your marriage. For example, we established very early in our marriage to never allow anyone, including our children, to sit between us. We wanted this to be a constant reminder of our oneness with nothing coming between us. Even though we have never discussed this with our children, it is interesting to see them position themselves so my wife and I can sit together. What boundaries can you establish that will help protect the unity of your marriage?

Enlist the help of other godly marriages to safe-guard your marriage. Seek advice from couples in healthy marriages. Over the years, we have gone to countless marriage conferences to get a marriage realignment, but nothing has been more impactful than the godly couples we sought out for guidance because they were doing something right in their marriages. You will be surprised at how humbled and honored a couple will be when you are seeking wisdom from their marriage. What godly couple can help your marriage grow in the areas you need most?

Heavenly Father, I want to thank You for my marriage. Lord, please help me see the ways I need to guard my marriage and give me the wisdom and courage to make the changes so my marriage can fulfill Your purposes and provide the godly atmosphere in my home to raise my children.

~ Emir A. Ruiz-Esparza, secondary principal

Valentine's Day

And now these three remain: faith, hope and love. But the greatest of these is love.

I Corinthians 13:13, NIV

~

An Acronym

V Valuable ♥ *Your spouse is valuable! Handle with care.* Proverbs 18:22—He who finds a wife finds what is good and receives favor from the Lord. Proverbs 31:10-11—A wife of noble character who can find? She is worth far more than rubies. Her husband has full confidence in her and lacks nothing of value.

A Attitude ♥ *Your attitude toward your spouse should reflect the love of Christ.* Philippians 2:5—Your attitude should be the same as that of Christ Jesus.

L Love ♥ *Love each other daily with eternity in mind.* John 3:16—For God so loved the world that He gave His only begotten Son, that whosoever believeth in Him shall not perish but shall have everlasting life.

E Encourage ♥ *Encourage each other and be each other's best friend.* Romans 15:5-6—May the God who gives endurance and encouragement give you a spirit of unity among yourselves as you follow Christ Jesus, so that with one heart and mouth you may glorify the God and Father of our Lord Jesus Christ.

N Near to God ♥ *Stay close to God in prayer and in the Word, individually and as a couple.* James 4:8—Come near to God and He will come near to you.

T Thoughtful ♥ *Be thoughtful with your spouse, in word and deed.* I Corinthians 13:4—Love is patient, love is kind. It does not envy, it does not boast, it is not proud.

I Integrity ♥ *Always communicate with honesty and integrity.* Psalm 25:21 — May integrity and uprightness protect me, because my hope is in You.

N New (fresh!) ♥ *Keep your relationship feeling sparkly and new.* I Corinthians 13:5—It [Love] is not self-seeking, it is not easily angered, it keeps no record of wrongs.

E Excellence ♥ *Love is the most excellent way, so cherish each other!* I Corinthians 12:31—And now I will show you the most excellent way .

Our loving God, we have these silly rituals to remind us to love each other and to make one another feel special. Valentine's Day, I know, causes a lot of people a lot of pain due to unmet expectation God, as Your people, help us to rise above the frills of the world's love and have the love for one another that is symbolized by the nail holding You on the cross. God, love can be so hard; yet, You have made us a way. Jesus, we cling to Your example. Help us to love You and one another better.

~ A teacher and mother of four

Love All

Do not judge, and you will not be judged. Do not condemn,
and you will not be condemned. Forgive and you will be forgiven.

Luke 6:37, NIV

~

His perfect love changed lives.

As a parent and teacher, I strive to live out this command from Jesus. Do not judge. Wow—that is a hard one, isn't it? Everywhere we turn we are being judged by the world's values. Do you drive the right car? Is your house big enough? Do you make enough money? Do you have enough friends on Facebook? When this is what we hear from society, it only seems natural to judge others by their appearance, who they hang out with, the sins they commit, and the lives they choose to lead, doesn't it? Jesus says flat out "Do not judge!" It is not our job to condemn.

Jesus calls us to love everyone just as He did. I look at His time here on earth and think, wow…that man hung out with everyone, including those who were not like him, those who were shunned. He hung out with the lepers, tax collectors, adulterers, prostitutes, and anyone else that was not popular at the time. He loved them all. Even in the midst of their sin, He just extended His love for them—period. His perfect love then changed their lives.

Despite the world's lessons, I hope to teach my own kids and all my students to love everyone without concern for their appearance, who their friends are, or most importantly, for the sins they commit. It is God's job to judge, not ours.

Heavenly Father, You know what a struggle it is for us humans to not judge others. Please be with me and help me remember the words of Jesus, "Love your neighbor as yourself." Help me remember to not judge or condemn others for their sins as I am a sinner and need Your forgiveness. Help me teach my students and sons not to judge, but to love others. Amen.

~**Coach Evans, elementary PE**

Purposeful Parenting

With this in mind, we constantly pray for you, that our God may make you worthy of his calling, and that by his power he may bring to fruition your every desire for goodness and your every deed prompted by faith. We pray this so that the name of our Lord Jesus may be glorified in you, and you in Him, according to the grace of our God and the Lord Jesus Christ.

II Thessalonians 1:11-12, NIV

~

Purposeful, not perfect, parenting! Since our oldest was off to a wonderful new chapter called "college," my wife and I took some time to clean his room. We had joked that he was simply off to education camp for the next nine months, but we both knew family transitions were in the journey ahead.

As we cleaned his room, the sword and shield he kept on his wall caused me to reflect upon our parenting. In that moment the Lord comforted me with His presence and reminded me of what He had called us to do early in our parenting. Like most, we wanted to be perfect parents, not making any mistakes with our kids. Thankfully, God gave us a different perspective. Instead of striving for this false notion of being perfect parents, God made it clear that He wanted us to be purposeful parents.

> **Purposeful, not perfect, parenting!**

The Lord and Josiah both know how many times we have botched it up over the years. Thankfully, God's love, grace, mercy, and forgiveness have covered and redeemed our parenting mishaps. Now our most significant contribution as parents moving forward lies in our prayer life for our son. II Thessalonians 1:11-12 is now on our bathroom mirror as a daily reminder to pray for him.

The sword will always be a reminder of his passage into manhood, and the shield a reminder that his faith in Christ must be just that…his faith, and not his parents' faith in Christ. We now believe a "man of faith" has left our house. We have not been perfect parents, but we have done everything we can to be purposeful parents. We still have the awesome privilege of raising two more godly men.

To God be the glory for what He has done and will do in our family's life!

Heavenly Father, Thank You for the awesome privilege of raising my children. Please help me to see that You are not looking for perfection in my parenting, but purpose-filled intention. Give me a vision of how to be purposeful with my children and equip me to live it out faithfully for Your honor and glory.

~ Emir A. Ruiz-Esparza, secondary principal

Reflections - Part 1

Hear, O Israel: The Lord our God, the Lord is one. Love the Lord your God with all your heart and with all your soul and with all your strength. These commandments that I give you today are to be on your hearts. Impress them on your children. Talk about them when you sit at home and when you walk along the road, when you lie down and when you get up.

Deuteronomy 6: 4- 7 NIV

~

Go to church with your children, spend time with them.

From an early age, I dedicated my life to Christ and did the best I could to please God. When my husband and I were raising our three boys, we tried to live our life according to God's Word. I wanted my words and actions to be an example of what it meant to love Him.

To continue in our knowledge of His love for us and to grow our relationship with Him, our family was involved in the church. I taught Sunday school and sang in the choir. My husband drove the church bus and picked up kids on Sundays to bring them to church. We wanted to emphasize for our boys the importance of giving back to the church and serving others. Today, I have such joy in watching my children bless others.

We made choices that required financial sacrifice but allowed me to have the most time at home with my children. I stayed at home until our youngest child was in third grade. I used this precious time to teach my boys the Word of God and His will for our lives. I know each family has different convictions from the Holy Spirit; it is important that parents listen for His voice and follow through as a united couple on whatever boundaries He may give.

Each school year brings a new flock of students and parents. I know parents entrust me to speak His truth. I have many conferences with parents looking for guidance and seeking encouragement. I share with them that the best way they can help their children is by going to church with them. Spending quality family time is so important. Parents need to know what is going on in every aspect of their kids' lives! By having family devotion time, everyone can hear each other's heart.

I challenge you to live life according to His Word. When it may get difficult, refer to the above verse. I constantly refer to this verse in my classroom; it helps all of us!

Thank You, Lord, for the commands You gave us to keep us safe, commands that reflect who You are as a loving Father. I love You with all my heart, soul, and strength. Thank You for always providing for our family. In Your precious name, Amen.

~ From the heart of Kathy Holt

Reflections - Part 2

Therefore if you have any encouragement from being united with Christ, if any comfort from his love, if any common sharing in the Spirit, if any tenderness and compassion, then make my joy complete by being like-minded, having the same love, being one in spirit and of one mind. Do nothing out of selfish ambition or vain conceit. Rather, in humility value others above yourselves, not looking to your own interests but each of you to the interests of the others.

Philippians 2:1-4, NIV

~

God has allowed me to become seasoned. I have had the privilege of raising my family and teaching for many years. I strive to partner with parents and share with them some valuable information I have learned over the years:

> When parents and teachers work together, children prosper.

- Children often have a different perspective of classroom situations. Communication between students, parents, and teachers is vital to a successful school year. If parents can communicate with the teacher as soon as a troubling situation arises, it will not fester. Then the teacher can more appropriately help the student.
- God has gifted all children differently. Just because students struggle academically does not mean they will fail in life. All of my children struggled in school at one point, but all of them are successful in what God equipped them to do professionally.
- Parents should always encourage their children to do their best—even past graduation.
- School activities are important to children. Seeing their parents in the audience and knowing they have parental love and support helps to create trust.
- Even with life being so busy, it is important that parents know what is going on with their children at all times. Going through the backpack for school information, talking with their child about school, and having family devotion time will help parents be aware of what their child is experiencing.

When parents and teachers work together in Christ, children prosper, and they have a positive example to pass to the next generation.

Lord, As Your children working together to build the body, may we be like-minded, having the same love, being one in spirit and of one mind. I pray that future generations will witness our will to walk in Your way and that their feet will travel the same path. Amen.

~ From the heart of Kathy Holt

Humble Parenting

For the LORD delights in His people;
He crowns the humble with victory.
Psalm 149:4, NLT

True Servant

Not so with you. Instead, whoever wants to become great among you must be your servant.

Mark 10:43, NIV

~

I am forever convicted to look past the flaws.

It is, at times, so easy to see the flaws and imperfections in others. I must confess when I first met Matthew, I saw just that. Matthew was placed on my team at the annual Memphis Work Camp. Every year more than four hundred teens from across the country, come together to paint houses in Orange Mound, a section of the inner city Memphis. Matthew had been born with birth defects and was unable to use his legs. He was destined to spend his entire life in a wheelchair. But, Matthew was there to serve me. I thought to myself, how is he going to work on these worn down old houses? How is he going to deal with this heat and humidity? Will he be able to endure the long days? Oh how God taught me a valuable lesson that week.

In the heat, the dirt, the weeds, Matthew sat on the ground. He scraped old paint. He painted cement stairs and wooden porches. He was drippy with sweat. He was tired. Yet neither the extreme heat nor the long hours of work defeated Matthew; he never gave up! I learned so much from my friend Matthew that week. He showed me how to truly serve. I saw his heart.

Now, I am forever convicted to look past the flaws and imperfections of my family, my children, my students, and my friends. Matthew showed me how to look through my Father's eyes; for that is how God looks at the potential and the heart of each of us. With God's prompting to open our heart and mind, we can truly see.

Dear Lord and Father, Open my eyes, open my heart. Help me to focus on the inner beauty and gifts of each person in my life. May I learn to encourage them to be the best they can be. May I see the blessing each one is in my life. Amen.

~ **Michelle Bacon, fifth-grade teacher**

New Girl

But he gives us more grace. That is why Scripture says:
"God opposes the proud but shows favor to the humble."

James 4:6, NIV

~

It was my first year of teaching. Actually, it was my first week with a classroom of kids that were all mine! One day that first week when we were out to recess, another teacher asked one of my students who her teacher was this year. The girl replied with certainty in her voice, "Oh, I've got the new girl." "New girl?" Not "the new teacher this year" or "the lady with black pants on over there." Any confidence I had went right out the window. My students should at least know my name, right?

Rejoice at a new opportunity to be humble.

Thinking back on it now, this humbling and slightly embarrassing experience was actually good for me. It reminds me that it is okay to be the "new girl" and not know all of the answers all of the time. This year, as the "new girl" I have had to ask a lot of questions. I have found that it is better to humble myself and ask someone who has experience than to be prideful and not get the answers I need.

Every journey has a beginning. The trick is to remember you are not taking the journey alone, but rather with our God and the fellow travelers He has provided us. Instead of despairing about being ignorant at every new beginning, let us rejoice at a new opportunity to be humbled and better embrace our God and the body of believers around us.

Lord Jesus, Please give me the strength and courage to ask for help from others. I want to be more like You every day. Please give me opportunities to be humble so that I can give you all the glory when I succeed. Amen.

~ Miss Schmidt, the new girl

Beautiful Vessels

Those who cleanse themselves from the latter will be interments for special purposes, made holy, useful to the Master and prepared to do any good work.

II Timothy 2:21, NIV

~

It was May of 1965 and Mother's Day was quickly approaching. My two sisters and I had saved $6.00 to purchase my mother a most extravagant, unforgettable present.

We headed to Mrs. King's antique shop, which was really an old storage room above her bookstore. We visited the bookstore often, and she immediately took us to the treasure storehouse to hunt for mom's gift. After searching for almost a half hour, our eyes fell upon the ultimate Mother's Day gift. It was a beautiful, purple hand-blown vase, and it was going to belong to our mother! We purchased the vase and hurried home to give it to her.

It is important that we are ready to be used daily.

Mom seemed to truly love the vase, but the three of us soon noticed that she never used it. It stayed on a hallway table filled only with a coating of dust. One day we asked her why she never used it, and she responded that the vase was made of very thin, fragile glass. She explained that she did not want to break her prized possession. Instead, she used the strong, clear vase that appeared often on our dining room table filled with lovely flowers. Our vase was beautiful, but it was not useful or practical.

Years later, I used the vase story to explain to my children about the importance of making ourselves a fit vessel for God to use. We may be very beautiful on the outside, but it is important that we are ready to be used daily by God because we are fit on the inside, always ready and available for the Savior to do His work.

Lord, Help me be a fit vessel for You to use at any time that You need me to do Your work.

~ **Donna Ambro, teacher**

Foolish Hiding

When they heard the sound of God strolling in the garden in the evening breeze, the Man and his Wife hid in the trees of the garden, hid from God.

Genesis 3:8, Message

~

I was going through yet another day of requesting my children to clean up their rooms before daddy got home. This ritual is usually an on-going process that drains any patience I started with when initially asking. From the kitchen I could hear my kids playing in my son's room instead of cleaning. As I walked through the hallway getting closer to his room, I stated loudly, "I sure hope my children are cleaning!" I saw them duck down quickly behind my son's bed, as if to hide from me.

Prioritize transparency.

The scene reminds me of Adam and Eve in the Garden of Eden. God requested of Adam and Eve to not eat of the forbidden fruit, yet they did. Immediately, their first instinct was to hide from Him, just like my twins hid from me. How like myself and humanity as a whole. Our instinct is to hide from God when we fail, despite the fact that He sees us wherever we go! My son and daughter really thought I could not see them hiding, but it was as clear as day! How foolish we are to try to hide from our Father when He already knows and sees all. Repentance instead of retraction should be our prayer.

It goes against our very nature to present our shortcomings to God instead of hiding them. The amazing concept of grace allows a complete covering of our sins when we bring them to our Savior.

Today, prioritize transparency with your children, husband, and ultimately God. Fight the instinct to hide and bring your sin to light. Allow the purifying power of God to provide true restoration.

God, I have the innate instinct to hide from You when I am imperfect. Forgive me for not coming to You first with my faults so You can cleanse me. Please God, renew me. Cause my first instinct to be to run to You and not away from You. Help me be a good example in this and all areas for my children and husband. In Jesus' name, Amen.

~ Mrs. Schueller, fourth-grade teacher

Worthy of Imitation

*Do not cause anyone to stumble, whether Jews, Greeks or the
church of God—even as I try to please everyone in every way.
For I am not seeking my own good but the good of many, so that they may
be saved...Follow my example, as I follow the example of Christ.*

I Corinthians 10:32-33; 11:1, NIV

~

In teaching kindergarten over the years, parents have brought to my attention that imitation is the best form of flattery. Several years ago, a student's mom informed me that one of her daughter's favorite pastimes was playing school. She would set up her instruction area with a glass next to her. When her mom asked her why she needed to have the glass, she answered, "Well, Mrs. Santon always has a glass of tea next to her when she teaches."

We are going to mess up.

While mom intended the story to be very flattering, it was actually very humbling. Our words and actions are always on display for anyone watching to see. Paul writes in his letter to the church in Corinth that they are to follow his example, as he follows the example of Christ. A beautiful example of Christ's perfect life is in Philippians 2:1-11.

Our children are especially impressionable. They are always watching and listening. Are our words and actions worth imitating? Would we be proud or embarrassed to know that they were imitating us accurately?

As sinful people, we are going to mess up, and even during those times, our children are watching and listening to see how we handle ourselves. Do we ask for forgiveness? Do we confess our sin? Do we right the wrongs we have committed?

Paul's instructions are bold; yet, we too should be imitators of Christ in all we do. We can pray that our words and actions lead people to a relationship with Christ, especially our precious children.

Lord Christ, Thank You for setting a perfect example for us and for humbling Yourself by becoming obedient to death--even death on a cross. I pray that we can be imitators of You and that our words and deeds would testify to Your love. In Your holy name, Amen.

~ From the heart of Sue Santon

Servant Leadership

Instead, whoever wants to become great among you must be your servant, and whoever wants to be first must be your slave just as the Son of Man did not come to be served, but to serve, and to give his life as a ransom for many.

Matthew 20:25-28, NIV

~

Growing up in a Christian home, I was able to see my mother and father emulate Christ as servant leaders not just as parents, but also within their marriage and their church. I appreciate the sacrifices that they made. There was no lesson lecture, but I learned the meaning of servant leadership through the routine actions that were mirrored year after year.

> I learned the meaning of servant leadership through the routine actions [of my parents].

Their church ~ To prepare God's people for works of service, so that the body of Christ may be built up (Ephesians 4:12). This means with Christ being the head of the church, the entire church body is served in the act of providing leadership. It is not just the church leaders who become acutely aware of their place at the foot of the cross, but all those within the body of Christ. As we continue to grow in our relationship with the Lord at our churches, we must also have a shepherd mindset of gathering/strengthening other sheep to further His Kingdom.

Their marriage ~ You, my brothers, were called to be free. But do not use your freedom to indulge in sinful nature; rather, serve one another in love Galatians 5:13. God shapes us for service through a variety of methods, including the challenges faced in marriage. A good marriage is not the king or queen shouting commands to each other, but two servants looking for ways to serve one another. This servant leadership occurs through genuine, transparent humility, knowing our roles as husband and wife.

As a parent you have an obligation to teach and live out truth, as the Bible reveals it. Although parents have the authority and power to demand, they can choose instead to motivate through love and to educate by example. Remember the explanation given by Jesus after washing the disciples' feet.

Heavenly Father, I pray that we can be a people, a school community, and a nation of servant leaders. We live in such a time where self comes first. Help us humble ourselves daily as we seek Your will in our lives. Help us to take off our airs of pride and serve others first. Just as You came to serve, I pray that we, too, will walk in Your example. Thank You for allowing us to be Your light of Truth through our hands, feet, and lips. I pray that we as a people, school, and nation will never forget where we started, grounded in biblical truths and constantly seeking Your face.

~ **Sarah Hardinger**, mommy and teacher

Mama Bears

Since He did not spare even His own son, but gave him up for us all,
won't He also give us everything else?

Romans 18:32, NLT

~

Every parent knows the feeling, like someone just stabbed you in the heart. Someone hurt your kid. For me, it triggered two conflicting impulses: Mama-grizzly mode and an empathy that was brutally painful. Your rational part realizes that every child is going to experience hurt feelings, embarrassment, even rejection. Someone has to be picked last. For every winning basket launched as the buzzer ends the game, there is a spectacular failure somewhere in his life. There is a first break up, an unkind word, or loss in her future.

Inoculate them early and often with the Truth.

But being a parent has very little to do with logic and everything to do with that fierce determination to protect them.

So, what does a Christian parent do when teaching them to forgive is the last thing we feel like doing? We inoculate them early and often with the Truth: we love them and Jesus loves them just as much when they mess up as when they get it right. And when we want to launch a full-out Mama Grizzly assault on the sorry excuse for a human who hurt them, we don't. We take a breath; we open our arms and our hearts. We give our pain and anger to the God Who sent His son to die for us, and we show them how to do the same.

Daddy God, We cannot wrap our heads around the supernatural love that prompted You to endure Your son's suffering on the cross for us, for our child, and for the one who hurt her. Please carry our pain, grief, and righteous indignation so that we do not add to today's hurt the scars of bitterness in our child's heart.

~ An educating mama bear

Raising Sails

*Trust in the Lord with all your heart and lean not on your own understanding;
in all your ways submit to him, and he will make your paths straight.*

Proverbs 3:5-6, NIV

~

Recently, I sat in a seminar where the speaker told a story about Hudson Taylor when he was first embarking on his missionary trip to China in a sailing vessel. While on this trip, the wind ceased to blow, causing the boat to drift dangerously close to a cannibalistic island. The captain, out of concern for his ship and crew, asked Hudson to pray for the necessary wind to get them back on course. Taylor told the captain that he would pray after the sails were raised. The captain replied in anger that he was not going to make a fool of himself by ordering the sails unfurled when there was not even a slight breeze. The missionary stood his ground, and the stubborn captain relented and raised the sails. Although he appeared foolish at first, the captain soon received the wind he so desperately needed. In fact, God sent such a gale that the captain had to ask Hudson to stop praying before they lost control of the vessel.

> Our job is to obey.

Sometimes God leads us in a direction that does not make sense or even makes us look ridiculous. Maybe God's purpose is to keep us from destruction as He did with Noah, who looked foolish building a ship with no water in sight; or maybe He is testing our faith to see if we will trust Him at any cost, as He did with Abraham, who was willing to sacrifice his son.

Regardless of the action to which He guides us, our job is to obey. The journey may hold confusion, but we can trust in the Lord!

Lord, Help me to teach my children, just as Noah and Abraham taught their sons, to humbly obey You even in the face of persecution and shame.

~ **Arlene Reed,** teacher

Intellectual Pursuit

We know that "We all possess knowledge." But knowledge puffs up while love builds up. Those who think they know something do not yet know as they ought to know.

I Corinthians 8:1b-2a, NIV

~

Intellectual humility is the heart of intellectual pursuit.

Paul is speaking about an arrogant group of "super" apostles who claimed to be smarter than Paul himself. Paul dispels the notion that they have a knowledge that is not common to everyone else-"We all possess knowledge." Paul's warning focuses on their arrogance in the way they treated others. He makes two key points: 1. The pursuit of knowledge without humility leads to pride and arrogance and 2. When you think you have arrived intellectually, you cease to learn. Intellectual pursuit begins with a teachable (humble) spirit and ends with an unteachable spirit. Even Jesus, who is called the wisdom of God, was humble even though he was the smartest man alive. If the great intellectual Jesus was humble, how much more should we be humble? Intellectual humility (a teachable spirit) is the heart of intellectual pursuit.

Dogmatic, unexamined beliefs are suspect and preclude listening to the opinions of another. God's truth invites all contenders and wins without fear of being tested. To pose questions because you want to know the truth is different than arguing with others because you think you are right.

Our students must make the faith their own. We must see both our own and their education as a life-long pursuit, open-ended (not having arrived) and with humility (teachability). This is godly, intellectual pursuit.

Heavenly Father, May we never become prideful or contentious in our opinions. Without being "puffed up" with knowledge, may we "speak the truth" in love, looking toward the welfare of others. O Lord, makes us as humble as Jesus, and it is in His name we pray, Amen.

~ **Dr. Thomas Reedy, teacher**

Poisoned Wells

~

Have you ever had roast preacher for Sunday dinner? Skewered youth pastor on a stick for lunch? Barbecued teacher? I have. Ironically, I was counting on those same menu items to partner with me to raise my kids in the "nurture and admonition of the Lord" (Ephesians 6:4).

Relate to others with humility.

Then I heard a sermon that really hit home. The title was, Don't Poison the Well from which your Children Drink. I realized I'd been dumping battery acid in my own family's water supply! I thought I was standing up for my kids, protecting them, the way my mom did. In reality, I had sabotaged the authority of committed folks who were pouring their lives into my kids.

I kept forgetting that children, even tall children with facial hair, are immature. Their perceptions, conveyed to me with great intensity, were often incomplete or inaccurate because of their limitations as, well, children.

The adults were not perfect of course, but neither were my kids. I had to learn to hear my kids out, show them I cared, but then follow up directly with the grownups involved without jumping to conclusions or dragging other people into the conflict. I was not very good at it. Honestly, my husband was much better at this than I was. Prying my hands off the controls so he could exercise his superior interpersonal skills – well, that is a subject for another day. Writing this, I wonder, would I have had to hand over that part of parenting if I would have learned better then how to respond to authority with a teachable spirit?

Jesus, Please help me relate to others with the humility You displayed. Give me discernment, grace, and wisdom.

~ Grandma Ruth

Developing Minds

*But in your hearts, revere Christ as Lord. Always be prepared
to give an answer to everyone who asks you to give the reason
for the hope that you have. But do this with gentleness and respect....*

I Peter 3:15, NIV

~

I have loved teaching 8th and 9th grade for many years. They enter so young, so naïve and feeling like they have all the answers. It is a pleasure to see so many with confidence in everything they have been told. Yet, a goal of mine is that they leave my classroom with an understanding far beyond that with which they had entered. I want them to have the same confidence in their beliefs, but I also want them to have a full understanding of what others believe. This understanding will allow them to have intelligent conversations with other believers who may not agree with them on every point.

We struggle to treat other believers with gentleness.

It was Christ's last prayer for believers that they be united, and yet we have failed miserably on this mission. We remain divided over the little things, and we struggle to treat other believers with gentleness and respect, so how can God expect us to treat non-believers with these qualities?

The minds of these young men and women develop so much in these years, and it is vital for them to have significant conversations with their parents, their teachers and other adult leaders that God has placed in their lives. Take the challenge of expanding the perspective of your child, searching for opportunities for growth.

Dear Lord, Give us wisdom to know how to lead our children. They are a gift from You, and we have such a responsibility to shape them. We humbly ask for your provision of a multitude of wise counsel for them as they walk out Your purposes.

~ **Wayne Stam, Bible teacher**

Opening Up

If my people, who are called by my name, will humble themselves and pray and seek my face and turn from their wicked ways, then I will hear from heaven, and I will forgive their sin and will heal their land.

II Chronicles 7:14, NIV

~

For a very long time, I have had the mentality that I have had to be perfect and that my past should have been perfect. Yet, since I am not; and my past is not, then I should keep that part of my life private. Having said that, I just experienced a breakthrough the other night while sitting in a car with two fabulous ladies. For three hours I told them all that I had been through and where God has brought me. I

God has blessed me in spite of myself.

always knew I had a testimony for Christ and that God had forgiven me, but it was that night that I felt forgiven by others in sharing myself with them.

I think too often we feel that we need to disguise the ugly part of ourselves, instead of claiming it as forgiven through the blood of Christ. It was nice to not be judged, but to claim it as a victory that God changed me. This was not my experience growing up. I think a lot had to do with my insecurities and feelings of inadequacy, but my sisters in Christ reminded me that God had covered my sin on the cross of Calvary.

Without divulging all details, life was tough. Due to pregnancy before marriage, my teaching days ended (for a season). I had no insurance, and no support from the person I needed it from most. However, the list of God's mercy and favor upon my life is such an amazing testament to the Scripture in Hebrews 13:5 that says, "I will never leave you or forsake you." He remained faithful, even through those rough times.

My full circle happened just two days ago when the prayers of this mother came to fruition. On June 26, 2010, God was good; and I married my best friend. Two days ago my son was recognized for writing an essay about what his father means to him. As I listened and watched them standing together on stage, my heart was overwhelmed with the goodness of God. He makes no mistakes, and in my weakness He is made strong. I can hold my head high, knowing that God has blessed me abundantly in spite of myself, in spite of my failures, and in spite of my poor decisions. Most certainly, He wants to do the same for you.

Father, I pray over those reading this today who need to forgive themselves of past wrongs. Help them to feel Your holy presence and everlasting love surround them today. I pray that they walk worthy of You, for You have created them in Your image, and You make no mistakes. In Jesus name, Amen!

~ **God's girl**

I Can

I can do all things through Christ who strengthens me.

Philippians 4:13, NKJV

~

All parents want their children to be successful in whatever they do in life. Therefore, the natural response would be to help them along the way as much as possible. One dear mother I worked with in the past very definitely felt this way and did as much as possible to help her very capable son. In the early years of elementary, she would see to it that all of his school work was done and personally get his books together and in his book bag before going to bed at night. He never had to be concerned about having his work ready or his books in class. Later in elementary, this very concerned mother would see to it that every problem in math was correct, even if she had to get the answer for him. After all, she wanted him to be successful. As he entered junior high and high school, he was very successful and won many awards thanks to his dedicated mother standing behind him all the way.

Have success through Christ, Who gives you strength.

In his sophomore year of high school, his mother became very ill and was unable to be there for him to be sure everything got done to guarantee his continued success. He quickly realized he was unable to organize his work or get his assignments done on time. He had learned to completely depend on his mom and had never learned that he could have success through Christ Who would give him strength.

Sometimes the best way we can help our children succeed is to teach them they must depend on God, not on us as parents. This release demands we parents lay down our pride and allow God to be in control.

Dear Father, Help me as a parent to always be available for my child and support him/her in every way possible, but never let me take away that dependence they must have on You. I know You are the only one Who can always sustain my child and take him successfully through life. Give me the strength I need to be the parent You want me to be. Amen.

~ Teacher

Critique

Don't pick on people, jump on their failures, criticize their fault—unless, of course, you want the same treatment. That critical spirit has a way of boomeranging. It's easy to see a smudge on your neighbor's face and be oblivious to the ugly sneer on your own. Do you have the nerve to say, 'Let me wash your face for you,' when your own face is distorted by contempt? It's this whole traveling roadshow mentality all over again, playing a holier-than-thou part instead of just living your part. Wipe that ugly sneer off your own face, and you might be fit to offer a washcloth to your neighbor.

Matthew 7:1-5, Message

~

Whether teaching in school or at home with my own children, I have encountered personality types that want to test every limit and types that want to follow rules as closely as possible. Some fall in the middle of the two extremes, of course. I remember teaching preschoolers and having multiple tattle sessions. A phrase I used to repeat often was "You take care of you and let me be the teacher."

It is hard to swallow instruction as an adult.

Well, there was an incident with a family member that really hurt my feelings during the time I was in my first year of teaching. I was able to so clearly see negative traits in my offender, and I wanted so badly for her to act differently! We have completely different personality types, so getting along had always been tough. I found myself talking to God about the way my family member mishandled the situation. I was tattling! Suddenly, God used my own phrase to school me. God spoke the words to me, "You take care of you and let ME be the teacher."

We teach children to listen to what we tell them, but it is hard to swallow instruction as an adult, especially when emotions are flying high. I swallowed my pride and began praying that I would start acting the way I should, instead of trying to tell God how other people should act. Although we may not agree with how other people treat us, our responsibility is to take care with our own words and actions. The only person we can change is the one that looks back at us in the mirror. God's got the rest.

God, You know my natural instinct is to be critical. It tends to be easier to judge others instead of myself. I know this is not Your plan for me or the people I come into contact with, so please change my critical spirit, Lord. Help me to build others up instead of tearing them down. Create in us a good example for our children in this area as well, God. Thank You for convicting us in areas needing Your guidance.

~ Jennie Schueller, fourth grade

Focused Eyes

Set your minds on things above, not on earthly things.

Colossians 3:2, NLT

~

In I Samuel the Bible tells of a young David. He is being hunted by Saul, the current king of Israel. David is presented with two separate opportunities to kill Saul, but he chooses not to act on either occasion. Instead of cursing King Saul, David refers to him as "the Lord's anointed." Nobody would have blamed David for defending his life by killing Saul as that would have been the natural human response: defend yourself. However, David did not have his eyes fixed on what mere humans would do in this situation; he was focused on what God's will was. David knew that God had placed Saul on the throne, and that it was not David's place to change that.

How far will I go to see that God's will be done?

Here we get to witness David submit to God's will, even when it may threaten his own life! Think about how radical that seems. Many of us pray the Lord's Prayer often and call to God, "may Your will be done." It is easy to mean this when God's will aligns with our own. But ask yourself, "How far would I go to see that God's will be done?"

It seems too often that life throws trials in our paths. In these situations, the natural response is to try to take control as quickly as possible. Inside the classroom is no exception. Throughout my first year teaching, I would have moments of feeling completely overwhelmed. I would feel as though I were putting everything I had into ensuring the success of my students, and then something unexpected and disheartening would happen. And the first thoughts that raced through my mind were, "What am I not doing?" "What do I need to change?" "Why aren't my students doing well?" "Maybe I am not a very good teacher." Having these immediate intrinsic thoughts would push me to create a plan to "fix" everything. However, when I responded this way, I left no room for God to work in the situation.

Ultimately, I have learned to trust the Almighty Lord. Actions should not be based on our intellect, but from God's still, small voice. If you pause to allow God to show you His will, His grace and mercy will abound all the more.

Dear Heavenly Father, May I always be seeking your will in my life, especially when trials arise. Please help me to surrender my own will to Your plan. May I live this day with the same faith, courage, and focus with which David lived. In Jesus' name I pray, Amen.

~ **Still-growing teacher**

Great Parenting

If you are wise and understand God's ways, prove it by living and honorable life, doing good works with humility that comes from wisdom.

James 3:13, NLT

~

I will never forget the days my children were placed in my arms for the first time. Suddenly, out of my whole being came forth the deep desire to be a great parent.

I can imagine that Mary, the mother of Jesus, felt the same emotions when her son was placed in her arms over two millenniums ago.

Great parenting comes from being obedient.

First of all, Mary was a parent of faith. Mary's relative Elizabeth says to her in Luke 2:45, "Blessed is she who has believed that what the Lord has said to her will be accomplished." I cannot imagine what must have gone through Mary's heart and mind when she first learned that she would carry, give birth, and raise the Savior of the world. Yet despite this surprise announcement, she accepted what was to happen in faith. We, too, can have this faith in our lives and in our parenting.

Secondly, Mary was a parent of reflection. No doubt there were many mind-boggling moments in the years spent raising Jesus. The Bible tells us in two places, "Mary treasured up all these things and pondered them in her heart,"(Luke 2:19)."But his mother treasured all these things in her heart." (Luke 2:51). Too often, as parents we find ourselves reacting and responding rather than reflecting.

Lastly, Mary was a parent of humility. It was not what others saw in her outward appearance, but instead what the Lord saw in her heart. She spoke of her humble state in Luke 1:48, "for he has been mindful of the humble state of his servant." She was just a young girl from Nazareth with no social status at all. Yet, Mary gave up her dreams, rights, and expectations, agreeing to serve Him humbly. She did not argue or push her own agenda, but submitted to God and all He had planned.

Mary's life reveals that truly great parenting comes from our being obedient to what God calls us to do, accepting His design for our life and the lives of our children.

Lord, thank You for giving me my child. I need Your help in being a great parent. I want to be obedient to what You have called me to in raising someone who loves and follows You. Help me cherish each moment. I am humbling myself before You and trusting that Your plan is perfect.

~ Mrs. Sanders, vice principal

Wise Parenting

But the wisdom that comes from heaven is first of all pure;
then peace-loving, considerate, submissive, full of
mercy and good fruit, impartial and sincere.

James 3:17, NIV

Walking Wise

Blessed is the man who walks not in the counsel of the ungodly, nor stands in the path of sinners, nor sits in the seat of the scornful; but his delight is in the law of the LORD, and in His law he meditates day and night.
He shall be like a tree planted by the rivers of water, that brings forth its fruit in its season, whose leaf also shall not wither; and whatever he does shall prosper.

Psalm 1:1-3, NKJV

Become wise by walking with the wise; hang out with fools and watch your life fall to pieces.

Proverbs 13:20, Message

~

Whom we choose as friends may be the most important choice we make.

We have all heard the saying "birds of a feather, flock together," or as I told my kids, you become like those you hang with. Whom we choose as friends may be the most important choice we make short of our decision to follow Christ.

As parents, we wanted our house to be the gathering place, the home where our sons and their friends wanted to spend time. This way, we got to know their friends… the kids they were hanging with. What kind of kids were they? What kind of families were they from? Did their values match ours? We wanted to know.

Making your house the gathering place is not always convenient or easy. I cooked endless pots of spaghetti and always had extras in the fridge. The remodel project had to wait as we put our time, energy, and resources into gatherings on the lake and ping pong tournaments. Date night gave way to hosting high school Bible studies and watching countless soccer games. We invested in our sons and their friends…and it paid off.

Now they are grown with families of their own. We have done the remodeling and best of all, every night is date night!

Dear Lord, Help my children to choose their friends wisely. Place friends and others in their path who are wise. Give them a discerning heart towards the character of others. Let them love Your Word. I trust You with my children, Lord.

~ Linda Harrelson, head of school

Intentional Living

I have brought you glory on earth by finishing the work you gave me to do.

John 17:4, NIV

Where there is no revelation, people cast off restraint . . .

Proverbs 29:18a, NIV

~

Facing death, Jesus told His Father He finished everything He was given to do in His life. This is a stunning, truthful admission. To come to the end of life regretting you have not done everything God gave you to do is a fate worse than death itself. How might this be avoided? We must live an intentional life for Christ.

> We can express our gift and calling anywhere.

Set intentional, godly goals and priorities. Finish the work God gave you to do. This means allowing the "revelation" (God's revealed will) to restrain (discipline) activities that are not important priorities. Urgent tasks are not necessarily important tasks. Daily demands cry out for our attention. Without focus we will drift along in worldly routines as life passes by. You must find out what God wants you to do every day; otherwise, circumstances, indolence, or selfish pleasures will set the agenda for your life.

You are on course when three things are true about your life: (1) you are obeying what God specifically told you to do, (2) you have disciplined your life to live by the values of God's heart (living by the Holy Spirit) in terms of character and relationships with others, and (3) you are faithful in exercising your spiritual gifts and calling as the Holy Spirit leads.

Once God has spoken we must obey, but we can express our gift and calling anywhere; however, whatever we do should reflect the character and values of Jesus. This is intentional living.

Lord God, May I intentionally live for You to transform my world and not be conformed by it. Amen.

~ Dr. Thomas Reedy, English

Life Goal

Not that I have already obtained all this, or have already arrived at my goal, but I press on to take hold of that for which Christ Jesus took hold of me.

Philippians 3:12, NIV

~

When I was in elementary school, my dad started asking me to write down my goals: goals in school, goals in sports, goals in Sunday school. Though at times I felt like my life was a Tony Robbins conference, I still thank my father for teaching me this important lesson: you cannot possibly hit a target at which you are not aiming.

You cannot possibly hit a target at which you are not aiming.

Years after my father's early morning motivational speeches, I became a theatre director. Much of my life now is spent helping students create realistic characters on stage. We ask questions ranging from the silly (what's my character's favorite cartoon?) to the existential (does my character believe in heaven and hell?), and everything in between. But the most important question, the one my students are sick of hearing over and over again, is "What does my character want? In this moment, this year, this lifetime?" In other words, what are his or her goals? My father would approve.

But so would our heavenly Father; His son Jesus was clear about His goals. In John 4:23 (NIV), He states his purpose: "...to do the will of him who sent me and to finish his work." He pursued those goals and accomplished them, and not because they would make friends and influence people, either. He followed his Father's goals, and He hit what He aimed at.

Father God, We thank You for teaching us how to follow in Your footsteps day by day, and we pray that You would help our children to run the race You have marked out for them with tenacity and courage.

~ Emily Stam, future mommy, theatre teacher and director

Spiritual Order

But I want you to realize that the head of every man is Christ,
and the head of the woman is man, and the head of Christ is God.

1 Corinthians 11:3, NIV

~

Sometimes, experience can be one of life's best teachers. Unfortunately, we must suffer the pain and consequences that result from choices made that did not align with God's instruction for our lives. As parents, we pray that our children will not have to suffer in the ways that we did and can learn from our counsel. Fortunately, God's given us a perfect instruction manual in His Word.

His blessings flow when we follow His intended order.

My children grew up in a home with a father who chose not to be a spiritual leader and suffered from alcoholism. We all lived with many consequences from his choices. In stepping up to be that leader for my children, I did everything I could to provide for them spiritually, but a part of the equation was still missing. I still weep with gratitude when I recall how the Lord provided Christian men to guide and counsel my boys. As our boys become men, they need to experience what it means to be a spiritual leader for their family, and our daughters need to be encouraged to find a man who will be the spiritual leader for their family.

Many teens have a difficult time understanding that life is not all about them. The world asks them to plan their life at a very early age. However, when they ask The Lord for His guidance in the decision-making process, they will reap many blessings instead of suffering consequences. Introducing our son to male mentors and instructing our daughter to begin praying for her husband can be very powerful. As a family, begin praying with your children for their future spouses and households.

What a perfect picture God has painted for us: God, Christ, man, woman. His instructions are quite specific, and His blessings flow when we follow His intended order. When men choose to be the spiritual leaders of their household and women show their husband honor and respect in the presence of their children, the entire family benefits.

Father God, Thank You for loving us in such a perfect way. May we always turn to You when making choices and decisions for our life. May we take the time to listen and know that when an answer to prayer does not appear to come, that it may not be the right time or that You have something better for us. Your plan for our life is the perfect plan, and for that, we are thankful. Amen.

~ A teacher

Special Gifts

Train up a child in the way he should go,
even when he is old he will not depart from it.

Proverbs 22:6, ESV

~

Trust God's sovereignty.

My children are polar opposites. I am third out of four children who are all wired differently. I have often been surprised by the drastic differences I find in the siblings I have taught over the years. We are all different, yet we are all created in the image of God.

Unfortunately, we sometimes forget that our job as parents is to nurture our children to become what God intended them to be. More often we want to make our children into our own image instead. It is an honest mistake. We tend to encourage what we know. It is hard for me as an extroverted, outgoing, expressive mother to affirm my shy, reserved, introverted daughter. It is not easy for my husband of few words to relate to our son who wants to tell every single thought and feeling of every single thing that happened throughout the course of the day.

In Psalm 139 we read that we are all "fearfully and wonderfully made." We must embrace the uniqueness of our children and let that help us as we decide how we are going to train them. We should discover their bent and affirm it.

As we guide our children, I think we must remember to trust God's sovereignty in the way He created them. God wired them the way He did in order to reflect a unique character quality from His personality. When we realize this, we will be better equipped to parent. This will be reflected in the way we discipline, motivate, disciple, relate, communicate, and serve them.

Father, I pray that You would give us wisdom to discover the uniqueness of our children and to affirm that they are exactly as You created them to be. May we be willing vessels to help accomplish Your destiny for their lives.

~ Trissa Lucht, choir teacher

Heavenly Thoughts

Then Jesus called for the children and said to the disciples, "Let the children come to me. Don't stop them! For the Kingdom of God belongs to those who are like these children. I tell you the truth, anyone who doesn't receive the Kingdom of God like a child will never enter it."

Luke 18:16-17, NLT

~

I have tried to talk to my three-year-old twins about Easter as the holiday was quickly approaching. I was sitting on the living room floor telling them that Easter was coming up in a couple of weeks. They saw me buy little Easter goodies at the store for their baskets, but as a believing mother, I wanted the conversation to go deeper than candy and the Easter bunny.

I wanted the conversation to go deeper.

Since they would not quite grasp Christ dying for us yet, I focused on the fact that we get to celebrate Easter because Jesus loves us. I told them that Jesus arose and went to Heaven. My son, Nathan, automatically said, "Mom, can we go to Heaven?" I said, "Yes, we will someday." He said, "In two days!" I, of course, said "Probably not two days, but soon…someday Jesus will come back for us, and we will get to go to Heaven. Jesus lives in Heaven, but he also lives in our hearts."

I have found myself being fearful of death. I am more concerned with who I would leave behind than worried about where my eternity will be spent. I am confident in my relationship with God and love thinking of Heaven as where I will go someday when I die at over 100 or when the rapture takes place, but my son's response to Easter was eye-opening. All he knew is that Jesus loves us, and Jesus lives in Heaven. He was ready to go--no fear and all joy!

Sometimes we get distracted with all the things going on in this world, forgetting we are only passing through to our real home in Heaven. Somehow we equate leaving this world as the end when it is only the beginning of our intended existence.

God, Thank You for showing me how my response should be to the mention of Heaven. You are there, and You love me. My goal on Earth should be to do the best I can to lead others to follow You before my eternity is spent in Heaven. I want it to be crowded with those who love You. Help me receive Your Kingdom as a child and love You in the most pure and simplistic way. In Jesus' Name, Amen.

~ Mrs. Schueller, fourth-grade teacher

Parent's Legacy

Train a child in the way he should go. When he is old, he will not turn away from it.

Proverbs 22:6, NIV

~

When I became a parent, it was the most exciting, yet scary, time in my life. There were no manuals, no guidebooks. God trusted me with this life that I was to mold, shape, teach, love, and provide for. It was and is scary. When I think about leaving a legacy for the kids in my life, including the hundreds that I come in contact with daily, these are the things I hope to instill. They will:

A legacy rooted in love will change lives.

- be the kids who stick up for the ones being bullied--no matter what that might mean to their social standing;
- grow up to be loving, respectful, gracious, and kind;
- be unnerved by the very thought of injustice, striving to do something about it;
- find something they love to do so much that it does not feel like a job;
- laugh every day;
- put others first;
- learn what it feels like to love children of their own;
- feel loved and appreciated for who they are; and
- come to know God so intimately that even when their faith is shaken; they will still trust Him.

A legacy rooted in love will change not only the lives of my kids, but also the lives of the people around them.

God, You left the ultimate legacy in Your Son, Jesus. I know that my legacy will never compare to that, but I pray that You will keep my heart rooted in love so I can leave a legacy that honors You. Amen.

~ **Coach Evans, elementary PE**

Treasure Wisdom

Be careful what you think, because your thoughts run your life. Don't use your mouth to tell lies; don't ever say things that are not true. Keep your eyes focused on what is right, and look straight ahead to what is good.

Proverbs 4:23-25, NCV

~

We are not just in the business of knowledge; we are in the business of wisdom. Knowledge is a good thing. It enables us to do our jobs, design, create, build, and maintain the goods and systems for modern life. But knowledge alone will only get us so far. With every generation, knowledge is becoming a fleeting and flexible thing. Much of the "knowledge" that we are teaching today will be obsolete by the time these children grow up and enter the workforce.

We must learn to not be overwhelmed by the ways of the world.

So, what are we to do? The answer is to seek wisdom. Verse seven of the same chapter of Proverbs says, "Wisdom is the most important thing; so get wisdom." According to Webster's, "knowledge deals with something learned and kept in the mind."[13] Wisdom involves making a judgment and being able to look beneath the surface for truth. Parents and teachers must work together to instruct our children in the eternal teachings of God. We also must study them in order to understand what He wants us to know. We must learn to judge wisely and not be overwhelmed by the ways of the world so that we can pass along our wisdom to the next generation.

Heavenly Father, Please help us to be wise. Let us be able to pass on to our children the truth of Your Word. Let us not be limited to being dispensers of knowledge, but let us embrace the fullness of Your light.

~ **Cheryl Patneau, high school foreign language**

History's Plan

"For I know the plans that I have for you," declares the Lord, "plans for welfare and not for calamity to give you a future and a hope."

Jeremiah 29:11, NASB

~

> **We can rest assured that the Creator has a complete plan.**

Ask almost anyone the question, "What is history?" and you'll get an answer that has something to do with the recorded past. As a Christian, I believe there is much more to it.

The first day of the school year I bring in a big box of dominoes and dump it on the floor. My new freshmen are challenged to build the greatest domino train ever conceived. They start having so much fun they forget they are at school! After launching their complex trains at the end of the hour, I give them the mysterious homework assignment of writing a thoughtful answer to the question, "How are the domino trains like history?"

The next day we discuss. Most will now say the dominoes are like one event leading to another. This is a true statement. However, I will ask them if their train could have ever set itself up. No. If you dumped dominoes out a billion times, they would never organize themselves. There had to be creative minds at work to make a train appear.

It soon becomes apparent to the students that each train also had a definite beginning point, a designed path, and a definite ending point. They are reminded to notice how even their seemingly random twists and turns were part of the plan. In fact, the outcome of the whole path – beginning, middle, and end – was known entirely in advance.

I want my students to know beyond all doubt that history is relevant and personal; that there is a design, order, and purpose for studying it. We can rest assured that the Creator has a complete plan for Mankind—for each human life—that takes into account His design for what has already been revealed, that which is still unfolding, and that which we have not yet seen (but can be secure in by faith).

Sweet Lord, Teach our children to see the path You have created for them to follow from before the foundation of the world. Let them know the beauty and meaning found in history because it is Your complete plan for the human race—for them—past, present, and future.

~ Greg Finch, 20-year teacher and parent

Blooming Flower

To everything there is a season, a time for every purpose under heaven: a time to be born, and a time to die; a time to plant, and a time to pluck what is planted.

Ecclesiastes 3:1-2, NKJV

~

A pink tulip sits at my desk, while outside we have snow and a blistering wind. It seems odd to have it there, so out of place. The blooms are opening up. Despite the fact that it is winter, my tulip has been forced into spring. The beautiful pink flowers are being forced to open by manmade greenhouses and temperature control. Naturally blooming tulips are fragrant and dot our yards with the colors of springtime. My sweet little blooms are odorless and working hard to perk up my desk of piled paperwork.

Let the bloom open naturally.

Young children remind me of the blooming flower. Each one blooms in their own time, their own season. Each is unique in the colors of their individual rainbow. The colors show through so beautifully when they are allowed to bloom in their own time.

Decades of teaching young children have afforded me many opportunities to talk and share with loving parents. Parents want the best for their children; but often do not feel completely confident in their decision about placing their child in the correct grade, especially when it comes to kindergarten. This question often comes with summer birthdays. Do we let the bloom open naturally, in God's timing, or force it to open?

Childhood is a precious gift; a special time to explore and discover, not to be rushed. God has a natural season for growth and development. Let us not rush it for our own agenda. God sends us the seasons, and each one is not to be rushed.

Father God, Thank You for the children You have placed in our care. May we see them through Your eyes and with Your love. Please give us Your wisdom in helping them to become the person You plan for them to be in Your perfect timing.

~ Mrs. Wayman, early childhood educator

Race's End

Do you not know that in a race, all runners run, but only one receives the prize? Run so that you may obtain it.

I Corinthians 9:24, ESV

~

Perseverance is a trait that needs watchful oversight within children. Perseverance does not come easily and is always at the price of the death of our fleshly desires. In our culture of "all things right now," educators know, perseverance is a fading virtue.

> **Serving others and achieving goals are the soil in which true perseverance can bloom.**

This virtue must be intentionally developed by providing children obstacles that are manageable with dedicated time and effort. Small lessons come in ensuring responsibility, for example, cleaning the whole bedroom or staying in those music lessons for the entire year. Over time, the bar can be raised to require your child's faithfully serving of another person or achieving an award that seems out of reach. Serving others and achieving goals are the soil in which true perseverance can bloom. It is important parents seek increasing opportunities where children learns that expending themselves is greatly rewarding. Those very lessons will come to mind as they run faith's course, which often involves climbing mountains!

Encouragement can be found in Scripture as so many times Paul reminds us to finish the race. Lots of people start races. Many make it to the middle. But the part that matters most, is the strong finish. As we parent, we do well to remember the same for not only our children but also ourselves. In the weary race of raising up a child who perseveres, look to the heavens. There, you will be reminded that the prize of finishing your task is eternal.

Lord, in this moment I am just so glad that I am not running alone. Thank You for encouraging me as I run, and as I teach my children to run. I love that your Holy Spirit gives the true breath of life in the hardest parts of my course.

~ Kimberlee Gill, academic dean

Failing Forward

*For there is hope for a tree, if it is cut down, that it will sprout again,
and that its tender shoots will not cease.*

Job 14:7, NKJV

~

One of the hardest things about being a parent is letting my kids fail. When both of my boys started walking, I wanted to follow around behind them and catch them every time they fell. But how would they learn to get back up if I kept catching them? My daddy heart wants to protect the emotional falls, too. My oldest son is shy and reserved and gets his feelings hurt easily. It breaks my heart when he comes home from school and says a friend was mean to him. You can see in his eyes and hear from his heart that it really hurts him. I want so badly to go to the offending child and to tell him to be nice! I want to grab that phone and call the parents and try to resolve the situation myself; but in reality, that solves nothing. Instead, I teach my son to stand in confidence and say things like, "I don't like it when you push me, please don't," because I know I cannot—and should not—always swoop in and come to his rescue.

> ...failure, with God's help, makes us stronger.

It is so hard to watch our kids make mistakes and be hurt by others, but we are doing them a disservice if we do not let them figure it out. If we constantly catch when they "fall" they never learn how to get back up. In Jeremiah, God talks about the good plans He has for us. Those words are not just for us; they are for our children as well.

Some of the hardest times in my life have brought me closer to God, and it makes me wonder if I needed those things so I would rely on Him more. When we fall or go through something tough, relying on God to get us through strengthens our relationship with Him. I think of God being our parent and watching us fall and fail and how hard it must be to let it happen and not step in and save us from all the pain. But He knows that if we turn to Him, we can handle any situation.

Are you trusting in God's plans for your children's lives? It is hard to watch them fall or fail; but know that failure, with God's help, makes us stronger and will help us prosper.

God, Please help me to lean on Your plans to bring growth to my children. Help me teach them to trust in You and seek You when they are hurting, needing advice, or have failed. Lord, despite the cuts that the world brings, help them grow strong in You. Amen.

~ **Coach Evans, elementary PE teacher & coach**

Pursuing Excellence

For the creation was subjected to futility, not willingly, but because of him who subjected it, in hope that the creation itself will be set free from the bondage to corruption and obtain the freedom of the glory of the children of God.

Romans 8:20, ESV

~

The problem with pursuing excellence is that it can kill your soul. The story of the world is full of people who pursued excellence, but did so out of vanity and pride. Jesus himself had many-a-row with academically astute, spiritually dead individuals. In fact, in Matthew 23 He heaps woe after woe upon the heads of people devoted to learning, achieving, and being good. Still, the Bible obviously does not call for a mediocre life. We are to be salt and light! We are to preserve and illuminate, maintain and redeem every corner of the world around us. This kind of intentionality requires a dedication to excellence. So, how do we avoid becoming like the law-obsessed, empty tombs that Jesus encountered?

> **Be devoted to achieving excellence.**

The person of Jesus is the answer to this dilemma. His work on the cross frees us from the law, and frees us to excellence. If we can be captured with a vision of what He has done in this world—rescuing it from darkness with His sacrifice of love, promising to it a future of newness and beauty—then we can spend ourselves with abandonment into making things new and good in the world around us. This requires that we be a people whose thoughts, energies, talents and affections are devoted to achieving excellence in every corner of our culture.

Father and Author of All, We thank You that because Christ died a sacrificial death, we are alive! We are amazed that this death also put all of earth on a path towards newness and beauty. You invite us to be a part of this work, but we can do it with joy and freedom because the ultimate battle has already been won. The restoration and redemption of this earth is not dependent on us, but it is rather a privilege. We throw ourselves into this work as the freest and most alive of people. We love You.

~ **Middle school teacher**

Unorganized Organization

So whether you eat or drink or whatever you do, do it all for the glory of God.

I Corinthians 10:31, NIV

~

I used to dream about being June Cleaver, running my household with precision and perfection. There I would be, vacuuming and dusting--all while wearing my 50's style polka-dotted dress, my hair curled and red lipstick on! Now, I realize that my definition of organization is heaps of clothes on the floor (separated of course), dishes washed as I am starting that night's dinner, and the HOPE of the dog "vacuuming" the floor after my toddler is done throwing her food down.

> I have accepted it is okay to not be perfect.

While organization is important, I have also allowed myself to hug my kids at night and listen about their day instead of cleaning my house. I have also made teaching my kids to help in our home a priority. My youngest son has to jump up on the dryer to turn it on, but seeing his accomplishment makes me smile, knowing his wife will be pleased one day that he learned how to do this.

In my classroom I tell my students that no one but God is perfect. I started telling myself that very thing, and I find that when I let go of this "June Cleaver" mentality then there is more enjoyment in my home because mom is "present."

Don't get me wrong, I find myself going behind my children and facing the silverware all the same direction and re-folding towels that are wadded up in the hall closet; but at the end of the day I have accepted it is okay to not be perfect. June probably would not agree, but I know the Lord is more pleased with my parenting than my perfect home.

So take the to-do list, Pinterest™ project, or whatever else is hindering you from interacting with your kiddos and toss it away. Your child will not remember those things that did not get done, but He will remember the time that you invested in them for Christ.

Jesus, Help me to be the godly parent that You have called me to be. Help me to make time with my children the utmost priority while I still have them in my home. May all I say and do be a reflection of YOU in me! Thank you for choosing me to be the mom of my kids. I am forever changed because they are mine!

~ Mrs. Gamber, elementary teacher

Independence & Dependence

The Lord is good to those who depend on him, to those who search for him.

Lamentations 3:25, NLT

~

Teaching our children to be independent but being dependent on Jesus at the same time is integral to their success in school and in life. As parents, we want to do everything for our children. It is important to teach them to be independent.

We can be confident that we have victory in Him.

One way to help your child be independent is to give responsibilities at home. The chores should be age appropriate and without any pay. Children should be taught that families work together to make the family successful. Most likely, your children will feel good about contributing! However, if they do not like it or feel good about helping, they still need to do it.

It is important for parents to set the rules and be in charge, not be swayed by emotions. Remember, the goal is for your child to be independent and successful. It is not always pleasant for the child to take responsibilities for personal actions; but if you want the best for your child, you will allow them to experience some discomfort. Discomfort could include teaching them how to get up when they have fallen or accepting consequences for their own actions.

Children need parents to help them understand that life will not always go the way they want it to, and then take the lesson further to instill that we can always depend on God to help us through our trials. Help them understand that some trials we face are a result of our own actions, and others are not of our doing but are allowed to bring us closer to God. If we are always "fixing" things for our kids, then they will not know how to call on Jesus for help, and they will not have the confidence to know that they can do all things through Christ who gives them strength (Philippians 4:13) .

Dear Jesus, Help me to know how to teach my child to depend on You. Help me to know that it is not healthy to do everything for my child or make life easier for them by trying to shield them from consequences from their own actions. Help me to teach them to take responsibility for their own actions and to rely upon You to help them in any situation they face. Help me to know how to lead and encourage them by letting them be responsible, yet dependent on Jesus, as they go through life.

~ Lisa Slagle, first-grade teacher

Little Eyes

I lead in the way of righteousness, in the midst of the paths of judgment: that I may cause those that love me to inherit substance; and I will fill their treasures.

Proverbs 8:20-21, KJV

~

Earlier this year my husband asked my son, "Were you a leader today at school?" My son's sad reply, "No, dad." He knew that his teacher had reported his lunchroom folly. He was surprised to hear daddy's answer to his admission. My husband answered, "Yes, you were, but you were a leader for wrong because of how you acted at lunch with your friends." Every action is a model.

> Daily, I need to look to the cross.

We often talk to our sons about being a leader in every situation. There are two types of leaders: those leading for what is right, and those leading for what is wrong. As Christians, we are called to lead others positively. I want my children to notice the kid who does not have a friend at recess and play with him. I want them to stand up when others are making fun of someone. We often ask our sons to lead in the right way, and in turn, it makes me think, how am I leading? How am I leading my sons? My students? My friends? Is my conversation leading people in the right direction?

Daily, I need to look to the cross and be the leader Christ wants me to be. It is humbling to know that my sons are watching my actions. My boys are watching what I do when I am frustrated. They hear my conversations when I am on the phone. They see how I treat their daddy. It is my job as a mom to lead them for what is right. Daily, I need to ask Christ for help with this.

What little eyes are watching you lead today? Are you leading for right or for wrong?

Jesus, Thank You for giving me Your example to follow. I pray that I will lead my family and students as You would. My life is yours, Lord.

~ Ashley Kates, fifth-grade teacher

Strength in Weakness

But he said to me, "My grace is sufficient for you, for my power is made perfect in weakness." Therefore I will boast all the more gladly about my weaknesses, so that Christ's power may rest on me. That is why, for Christ's sake, I delight in weaknesses, in insults, in hardships, in persecutions, in difficulties. For when I am weak, then I am strong.

II Corinthians 12:9-10 NIV

~

True confessions: I do not like my child to fail—at anything. Somewhere along the way, I decided I needed to protect my child from failure at all costs, lest his feelings be hurt, or his class projects not look perfect, or he have any reason to be disappointed.

Our sovereign God is going before my child.

A couple of years ago, one of my child's very loving teachers encouraged me to help my child most by letting him fail. It was a year of pruning for both of us. Though it was a painful year in many facets, it was also extremely rewarding because I watched my child, who was dependent on his mom bailing him out in times of need, become more dependent on Christ for strength to endure difficult situations. We went to a Christian bookstore and purchased a cross that he kept in his desk with Phil. 4:13 on it. When he was in the middle of a hardship, he called on Jesus, not Mom to bail him out.

What a blessing it is to be able to look back on that school year of numerous failures and much weakness with sheer joy because my child is able to boast about what God did in his life. Sometimes, I catch myself wanting to rescue him from a painful situation or jump in and help him with an assignment that is particularly stressful. But, to do so would be to rob him of the sheer delight he finds in the Lord.

When I hear my dear child call on the Lord through prayer, I still get emotional. He deals with disappointment, his projects may not look perfect, and his feelings are sometimes hurt, but he has a growing confidence that only comes through the power of Christ working in and through him. Our sovereign God is going before my child, preparing the way for him.

Lord God, Your grace is sufficient for both my child and me. While I do not like my child to experience the pain of failure, I know that You are using this weakness to make him stronger. I praise you for your sovereignty, and I thank You for Your perfect plan. Thank You for using Your servants to remind me of Your promises!

~ **Alethea Beasley, communication arts teacher**

Biblical Parenting

I love them that love me; and those that seek me early shall find me.

Proverbs 8:17, KJV

~

The sooner people find Jesus as their personal Savior, the better off they will be. The world will not have had as much time to harden them and affect them as an unsaved person. I believe it stands to reason that parents should have a clear plan/vision in place to have their children seek the Lord early and become everything that God wants them to be.

Embrace every opportunity to share.

This plan/vision should always have in mind Proverbs 22:6, which says, "Train up a child in the way he should go: and when he is old, he will not depart from it." This training involves discipline. Consider Proverbs 29:17-18, KJV, "Correct thy son, and he shall give thee rest; yea, he shall give delight unto thy soul. Where there is no vision, the people perish; but he that keepeth the law, happy is he."

Here are six steps to help get your child to find the Lord early and fulfill Proverbs 8:17.

Step 1 — Instill discipline into your child and it will develop into self-discipline.
Step 2 — Build a relationship with them daily; communicate with them.
Step 3 — Have daily fellowship with them and the Lord.
Step 4 — Teach them responsibility and hold them responsible.
Step 5 — Serve the Lord in ministry together.
Step 6 — Talk about deciding to have Christ as Lord of your life, inviting your child to do the same.

Remember parents, your children are watching you live your faith. Embrace every opportunity to share it with them.

Dear Lord, Please help parents with the ever-important task of raising their children to find You, love You, and serve You. Please help parents realize that they have to model what the Bible teaches daily. Please give them the strength to do this Lord so that their children will find You early, love You, and serve You. Amen.

~ **Matt Shelton, secondary mathematics teacher**

Patient Parenting

… and patience is better than pride.
Ecclesiastes 7:8b, NIV

Overcoming Anger

He who is slow to anger is better than the mighty,
and he who rules his spirit than he who takes a city.

Proverbs 16:32, NKJV

~

"You did whaaat???!!!" So goes the echoing cry of every parent everywhere at some point in their child's development. In that moment it seems every bit of hard won peace, joy, and righteousness flies right out the window.

In the fleeting moment after *the incident*, we also have a choice. Either we exercise discipline that disciples or punishment that destroys. Below are some "field-researched" tips from this old educator to ensure our actions as parents bring about instruction rather than increased frustration:

> **You are specially chosen to be God's image to your child.**

Remember — *Breathe in/Breathe out.* Repeat until blood pressure lowers. Not addressing the issue until heart rate is normal will ensure everyone's survival! Never try to discipline while angry.

Remember — *Maintain perspective.* There is nothing new under the sun. Just as we so often choose our sin despite a loving, nurturing heavenly father, so our children will, at times, exercise their free will to choose wrong. We should continue to view our child as God views us: worthy of discipline and unconditional love.

Remember — *God has equipped you.* That equipping does not necessarily mean that you won't need to call in reinforcements from time to time, but it does mean that you were chosen to be a key warrior battling for your child's spiritual health. Parenting automatically drafts you into seeing incidents through until there is resolution. You are specially chosen to be God's image to your child.

When *"whaaat"* happens, you are the one called to walk your child through the valley back into His perfect peace, joy, and righteousness.

Dear Lord, Thank You for my children. Though at times I feel my head may pop off because of their actions, I know they are Your great blessing to me. Help me to always keep my mind fixed on You so that I can lead them in the way that they should go. Grant me peace that passes understanding when their childish sin overwhelms me. And Lord, forgive me for my own moments of rebellion; I long for Your correction. God, make us a family in which Your heart rejoices.

~ Mrs. Gill, mom and 25-year educator

Carry Through

Children, obey your parents in the Lord, for this is right. "Honor your father and your mother" (this is the first commandment with a promise), "that it may go well with you and that you may live long in the land."

Ephesians 6:1-3, KJV

~

We have all heard the story of the foolish boy who cried wolf. After he had called "wolf" so many times, the townspeople did not believe him when he actually had a wolf in his flock of sheep. The consequences were deadly for his sheep. We have also heard about the parent who said to the children causing trouble in the back seat of the car, "If you do not stop right now, we will turn around and go back home" when they had no intention of going back home. This is the same foolish scenario of the boy calling "wolf." The children do not stop, and they soon learn that what a parent says is probably just an idle threat.

It is our responsibility to teach that obedience.

These may be extreme examples, but as parents we often do make threats that we know we will not, or cannot carry out. It is very important that when we tell our children we will do something that we carry through and do it. They learn quickly and will start calling the bluff. Then our children will not learn obedience to parents. According to Ephesians 6:1-3, our children are commanded to obey; and it is our responsibility to teach that obedience.

Unfortunately, this is not the biggest problem that results from telling our children one thing and doing something differently. We as parents represent God to them. Children begin to understand their relationship with God based upon their relationship with parents. They will soon assume that God also does not mean what He says in His Word. As our little children become adults they will have the idea that when God says "Thou shalt not..." that He does not really mean it. They will believe that there are really no consequences for disobeying God. To be consistent and do what we say we will do just might be one of the most important things we can do to help us teach our children that God also means what He says in His Word.

Dear Father, Help me to be consistent in what I do and say. May I never threaten or promise my children things I do not mean or I cannot enforce. Help me always discipline my children in a way that draws them closer to You. Give me courage and wisdom to make my children understand that You mean what You say in Your Word. Thank You, Father, Amen.

~ Teacher

Mismatched Shoes

Come to me, all you who are weary and burdened, and I will give you rest.
Take my yoke upon you and learn from me, for I am gentle and humble in heart,
and you will find rest for your souls. For my yoke is easy and my burden is light.

Matthew 11:28-30, NIV

~

Slow down and enjoy the moment.

Backpack...check! Lunch box...check! Breakfast on the go...Check! Full tank in the car...nope!

It is 7:00 AM, and Mom's Taxi Service has already had its first setback. "No problem," you say to yourself. "It's still early, and I have time to stop and get some gas." You pull up, get gas, and decide to treat your sweet daughter to her favorite nutritional snack of a chocolate doughnut. Big mistake! Besides the previously unnoticed uncombed hair and wrinkled pants, your daughter now has chocolate frosting on her white dress code polo. Oh well, still thinking positively, you tell her just to put her sweatshirt over it. She willingly agrees, and she proceeds to enjoy the rest of her nutritional doughnut. You pull up to the school building, rush her into the door to her classroom; and you soon realize that although she has everything she needs to start her day, you do not. Your work documents, lunch, and workout clothes are still sitting neatly on the counter where you had laid them out the night before. UGH! There goes the positive attitude you had started the day with. You suddenly feel the frustration creeping into your mind. How will you choose to react? Stop and think about the following questions: Is it worth spending my time getting upset over? Can I laugh about this? What is God trying to tell me through this situation?

Many times God is telling us that we need to slow down and enjoy the moment. Often times my favorite stories I tell my students have come from a stressful moment. I will never forget the morning that I dressed in the dark. I really felt put together until the end of the school day. One of my prize pupils happily pointed out, at the end of the day, that I was wearing two different shoes...one brown and one black. I am sure in that moment I was horrified, but it has now become a favorite memory of mine. It shows that we are human and are not perfect. My challenge to you is to climb outside of your box...relax... wear two different shoes!

Dear Lord, Thank You for my imperfections. Thank You for the stained shirts, forgotten papers, and mismatched shoes. You know my heart and desires. Help me to remember how to react in stressful situations. I want to leave a legacy of love.

~ Becky Flowers, sixth grade teacher

Little by Little

*And the LORD your God will drive out those nations before you
little by little; you will be unable to destroy them at once,
lest the beasts of the field become too numerous for you.*

Deuteronomy 7:22, NIV

*But I will not drive them out in a single year, because the land would become
desolate and the wild animals too numerous for you. Little by little I will drive
them out before you, until you have increased enough to take possession of the land.*

Exodus 23:29-30, NIV

~

God has our back, just like He did the children of Israel. In our minds, we know that, but do we really believe it in our hearts? Both accounts of this story state that God promises the children of Israel that He will drive out their enemies as they go into the Promised Land. The Lord is making it clear that it is His battle, not theirs. But look how He is going to do it: Little by little, lest the beasts of the field become too numerous for them.

We often pray for God's blessing in our lives as well as His protection and intervention on our behalf. Scripture is full of assurance that God does want to both bless and protect us. But often we have a problem with the way God works. We either want it now, as I am sure the children of Israel did when they had to wander in the wilderness for forty years, or we do not trust Him with our hopes and dreams.

These verses identify a life principle that we need to understand and teach to our children: God is all-knowing and all-loving. He wants the best for us and will give us only what we are ready to handle. Little by little. He knows that with each step, we will face a different enemy, another obstacle, a new set of problems. But each victory builds our faith and prepares us to face the next situation.

I think of David. He knew at a young age that he was to be king. What he did not know was that there would be many years before it happened. Those years were spent in preparation and fighting the enemies that could prevent success as king. I think of Esther. God had a plan to use Esther to save His people and used difficulties in her life to get her ready "for such a time as this" (Esther 4:14).

We must have patience. Little by little, we will overcome.

Dear Lord, I know You have my world in Your hands. Thank You for going before me to fight the battles. I know victory is assured. Help me have Your patience that I may trust in Your perfect timing.

~ Linda Harrelson, head of school

Do Something

I said to myself, "Relax and enjoy yourself because the Lord takes care of you."

Psalm 116:7, NCV

~

There are four minutes remaining on the microwave timer. What to do, what to do!? I must get something done! Should I empty the dishwasher, wipe down the countertops, run the broom over the floor, go to the bathroom???

If this is you, you are smirking right now, aren't you? Are you a person who has the insatiable desire to always "do something"? Yep, me, too. You live by the adage, "Idle hands are the devil's playground." Dare I say that overly busy hands/minds are also a play place for the devil? If you are in the habit of trying to fill every "free moment" with something useful I encourage you to reread the story of Mary and Martha (Luke 10:38-42).

Wait for God to speak to you.

For years I secretly agreed with and admired Martha. Just "sit and listen?" Come on, Mary, get up and do something! Only recently have I come to the realization and acceptance that Martha was truly missing out. Though the dishes would always be with her, her Savior would not.

Next time you have a few minutes left on the microwave timer, just relax (it will take practice). Keep a devotional or Christian inspirational book in the kitchen cabinet. Read a little while you wait. Sit (okay, or stand) still and wait for God to speak to you. Resisting the urge to "do something" is rough, but relaxing and enjoying yourself (because the Lord takes care of you) will be very rewarding.

Dear Jesus, When I am propelled to just "do something," remind me to relax and assure me that You will take care of me. Help me understand that I could very well miss out on a very specific blessing from You while I am "busy." Forgive me when I fail to wait for You. In Jesus' name, Amen.

~ Mrs. Busy @

Thorny Sticks

And let us not grow weary of doing good, for in due season we will reap, if we do not give up.

Galatians 6:9, ESV

~

I remember as a small child watching my parents plant three scrawny bushes comprised of sticks that were each about eighteen inches in length. However, these were no ordinary sticks. They were covered with the fiercest looking thorns my young eyes had ever encountered. For weeks I watched my mother give these thorny sticks tender loving care. I did not understand what all the fuss was about until the most beautiful red roses began to bloom. They were by far the loveliest, most fragrant flowers in the garden.

There is a "rose" in there somewhere.

Over the years, I have come to view some of my students as those thorny sticks. As such, I have a good work before me! There is a "rose" in there somewhere, buried beneath the veil of thorny behavior and prickly attitude. With enough prayer, love and encouragement, I know I will see the beauty God has planted within that child grow and bloom. I have encountered many challenging students in my twenty-four years of teaching. There have even been a few children I felt like giving up on, but God would bring to mind those thorn bushes to help me stay the course of loving them and seeking His wisdom in ministering His love to them.

If you are dealing with a "thorn bush" right now, do not give up! Somewhere in there is a beautiful rose lying dormant that just needs your "miracle grow" to bloom.

Lord, Please give me the strength and wisdom to say and do what is necessary to nurture the plants You have entrusted to me. May I see each child as You see them and love them as You do. Thank You for the privilege of tending Your garden and watching Your precious roses bloom.

~ Arlene Reed, teacher

Red Light

The heavens declare the glory of God, and the sky above proclaims his handiwork.

Psalm 19:1, ESV

~

Sometimes we need a stop light.

It seems like whenever I am in a hurry every light all the way to my destination is red. And I sit. And wait. And grumble. And complain.

There for a while, it felt like it happened every day before school. The light would finally turn green, and my patience had worn so thin I would floor it up the on ramp and arrive at school angry and adrenaline-filled.

All this wasted energy, until one day I made a pact to listen only to Christian music anytime I was in the car alone. Now, it was not that Christian music was not on before, because most of the time it was; but now I was going to really listen.

When you stop rushing through your day and take time to just listen, there is a lot to be seen and heard. God created so much for us if we would take the time to notice. The beautiful sun starting to peek over the hill, little squirrels scampering through the neighborhood, and even the sweet, soft voice of a small child singing along to every word in the backseat are each in place to soothe a ruffled soul.

Spending a few extra minutes sitting at the stop lights no longer bothers me because I started using the time to join my radio and praise God, marveling at His creations. It even helped me stop judging the man who set the timer on the lights. So maybe it was a good thing that I got stopped at those lights. It helped me realize sometimes we need a stoplight in our day to tell us, "Hey, slow down and look at all the great things that God has done for you!"

Dear Lord, Thank You for slowing my day down so that I can see all the awesome things that You have created for us. Thank You for teaching me patience and giving me a better attitude in the morning so that I can get to work and let Your light shine through me. Help my kids today slow down to see Your creations.

~ Coach "Ammo" Siemsen, PE teacher, Soccer coach, and mom

Traveling Circus

Therefore, my beloved brothers, be steadfast, immovable, always abounding in the work of the Lord, knowing that in the Lord your labor is not in vain.

I Corinthians 15:58, ESV

~

One, two, three car seats! Oh no, the buckle is stuck! The Dora backpack, the princess one, and do not forget the camouflage one with the late book report. I think I forgot to make lunches before I went to bed. Should I make them or tell my kiddos they "get" to have hot lunch today? Snow boots and mismatched gloves--is the snow coming today or tomorrow?

> Together, in grace and faithfulness... we will get our children through.

NO, we are not stopping for McDonalds. It is unhealthy and too expensive. Grab a juice box and a granola bar. Nope. No cereal. I forgot to have Dad stop and get milk on the way home. I know you do not like granola bars, just today, okay!? EAT IT.

My, oh my! It is almost 6:30. I have a really important meeting this morning. No dear, my job is not more important than you are. But my class is depending on me, and I want to be faithful to all of you. I want to give my best to them and show them the love of Jesus. Oh Yes, reminder, Jesus loves you, too.

And so it goes.

Our families are probably very similar. We struggle to find the balance while giving our all to those we love. I will remember when your kiddo forgets their socks for "Silly Sock Day" or leaves their hat at school for the third time this week. I ask that you remember when I forget about Show and Tell until it is nearly time to go home and when I forget to send home the paper you asked for.

Together, in grace and faithfulness to His call, we will get our children through!

Dear Lord, Please help me find the right balance in my life. I desire to serve You with complete faithfulness, but sometimes that service is a bit messy. Thank You for Your eternal grace. Help me to embrace it and strive daily to be more like You. Amen.

~ **Mrs. Wayman, early childhood educator**

Four Actions

We urge you, brethren, admonish the unruly, encourage the fainthearted,
help the weak, be patient with everyone.

I Thessalonians 5:14, NASB

~

Have you seen the cartoon of the teacher saying to parents: "Your kid was my favorite student to have absent." It might be a funny cartoon, and you might sometimes feel glad to ship your energetic child to school for several hours! But, is that a biblical mindset to have?

Remember love is patient.

The Bible says that we should "admonish the unruly." So, the teacher should not just stick him in the corner of the room by himself every day? So, the parent should not put on a *Gone with the Wind*-length movie for eight hours every day after school just to keep the kids quiet? No, the Bible says "admonish." Admonish the compliant? No. Admonish the average kid that no one can dislike because he is just a likeable guy? No. Admonish the unruly.

The Bible says that we should "encourage the fainthearted." This sounds a little more fun than admonishing the unruly! But, what if the "fainthearted" is faint of heart 180 of 182 school mornings? The Bible says we are to encourage that person. What if his or her faintheartedness makes me to be fainthearted? Encourage without fail; it will probably bring you encouragement to do so.

The Bible says that we should "help the weak." This sounds like a good, Christian thing to do. Something that will get us star stickers in heaven for sure! What if the "weak" is your child or the student I am responsible for in class? Star sticker or not, help that person! In weakness, God's strength is made perfect.

The Bible says that we should "be patient with everyone." Everyone? Yes, everyone! You mean that kid who will not sit down at his desk or the dinner table for more than thirty-seven seconds? Yes, everyone! You mean the kid who asks you seventeen questions, not a day, not an hour, but a minute! Yes, everyone! Remember love is patient. And the greatest of these is love. And God Himself is love! Be patient!

Dear Patient Heavenly Father, Thanks for being patient with me. You are patient at Your inner core. Help me to have a little of that patience today. Help me to give out what I have been given by You! I cannot do it on my own, but I can do all things through You and Your strength!

~ Six-year educator

Planning Patience

May he give you the desire of your heart and make all your plans succeed.

Psalm 20:4, NIV

~

Life takes a little planning. Sometimes the planning can be exciting: going on vacation, saving for a new car, or a date night without the kids! More often, it is an awful burden: dinner after school, doctor's appointments, or getting the kids to and from practice. Life can be a grind, and it is hard to be patient in the midst of trying moments, however well we plan for them.

God is confident in His plan.

I believe all of our families would benefit tremendously if we were more purposeful at planning ahead. We tend to be much more loving and caring people when we follow a plan. On the contrary, we are generally rude, short-tempered, and critical when we have no vision and feel the stress of life. Have you ever considered the connection between planning and patience?

God's plan for our lives--and for the redemption of the world--is a wonderful example of this connection. His plan goes back before you and I were born, beyond the creation of world. He knows each of us and has a very personal plan for our lives. He even knew we would each need a Savior.

So, when Adam sinned, when we sinned, it did not surprise God. He knew it would happen. He planned on it.

More than anything, I want my children to obediently follow their Savior. For this to happen, I feel like I must first be a living, breathing example of patience in their lives. I do not want to blow up at bath time when my girls make a mess, or lose my temper when bedtime is going terribly. Planning for these moments helps me be more patient in the midst of them.

God is confident in His plan, and He is confident in us as parents. Remember the plans you have made and stick to them. You may be surprised how much more patient you are!

Dear Lord, Please help me trust You. I know You are a good God, and Your plan for my children is perfect. I want to be a model of patience for them. Amen.

~ **Mr. Welch, third-grade teacher**

Beautiful Affliction

My brethren, count it all joy when you fall into various trials, knowing that the testing of your faith produces patience. But let patience have its perfect work, that you may be perfect and complete, lacking nothing.

James 1:2-4, NIV

~

Sometimes we find ourselves walking through trials of life both large and small. These trials or valleys are sometimes not expected or self-inflicted, but what we do with them can shape our character, future, and walk with the Lord. Indeed, there can be sweet fruit from sour times. Do not despair; God has a plan!

God's process for preparing us to live fruitful lives:

Burn off — God can allow us to go through the fires of life to burn off unfruitful parts of our lives. While the pain is real; it is temporal. The good it brings will be eternal. Romans 8:28

Break up — We cannot be fully blessed until our hearts are fully broken. In some cases God is tilling our hearts to break to break up that which is hardened. Then, with a humble (fertile) heart, we can grow la life bearing His glory rather than one of self-pity or self-idolatry.

Raises us — When we allow Him to raise us up, He is able to grow new, fresh fruit that glorifies Him.

There are always two agendas in the trials we face in life: God's and Satan's. The very trials that Satan wants to use to destroy you, God will use to reward you! Genesis 50:20

Thank You, Lord, for the valleys of life. While trials are hard, I am thankful they are not in vain. Thank You for humbling me so that I could truly see what it means to rely on and have a relationship with You. You are no more just a Sunday school story, but rather my heart's desire. I yearn to grow closer to You through the mountain tops and valleys, come what may. Thank You for wrapping me up in Your arms of love and grace when I run back to You. Thank You as well for the people You have placed in my life that speak Truth, even when it is hard to hear. Please help me to be bold enough to minister to others as they face similar trials.

~ **Sarah Hardinger, mother and educator**

The Surface

Deep calls to deep in the roar of your waterfalls;
all your waves and breakers have swept over me.

Psalm 42:7, NIV

~

It is a strange world that we live in today. The sun comes up; and we are off to the races with work, sports, meetings, games, and much more. With the fast-paced world we live in, we find ourselves just scratching the surface.

In my own opinion, this is the difference between a good teacher and a great teacher. A teacher's day is a schedule set to the last minute. We hear a bell multiple times throughout the day which insists students rush in and out of our class. So here is the problem: how can you not just scratch the surface?

> Jesus, the perfect teacher, never scratched the surface.

It seems impossible to actually stop and hear what is really going on. Every student needs a teacher that is willing to stop from the crazy schedule and listen. You can be known as a nice person by just scratching the surface, or you can be one who makes lasting impact. How my heart longs to be that teacher.

Jesus, the perfect teacher, never scratched the surface. In every story we see Him, he speaks to the heart, digging deeper with the people that needed it the most. He paused in the crowd to see who touched Him. He left his rest to calm fears in the storm. He sat and held the children. His love went beyond the rush of the moment to meet the need.

With God Himself pausing during the pressure of the daily rush, shouldn't we be challenged to do the same?

Lord, I pray that You will transform the experiences that You put in front of us. We miss out on so much, and I pray for the patience to slow down and dig a little deeper! Amen.

~ **Coach Bell**

Missing Out!

A man's heart plans his way, but the Lord directs his steps.

Proverbs 16:9, NKJV

~

I remember when I was younger I was doing exactly what this verse talks about: planning out my life. I developed this wonderful plan of what I envisioned life to be. I planned to go to college, meet my perfect man there and get married. Then, get the perfect teaching job, have children (one boy, one girl), be a cool mom, and have the best house. Then what happens? God leads us on our journey of life in a different way.

Learn to live in His presence.

We think we can control and guide our lives and completely forget that it is the Lord who determines our steps. For me, this planning did not stop with college. Oh no, repeatedly, I readjusted and reconfigured my plan. If asked whether I wanted God's will for my life, I would heartily and immediately answer, "Yes!" But what I started to realize was that my mouth was saying yes, but my heart was saying "No, Lord, that is not what I want for my life. No, that is not where I want to be." In the midst of my dreaming, wishing, and praying furiously, I had completely forgotten that I am on a journey led by my Jesus. I have a personal relationship with the God of this universe, and I am to be satisfied in Him and in His plans for me.

The Bible has some pretty good examples of some people who did this very thing. Remember the Israelites in the Old Testament, the ones God delivered out of slavery in Egypt? On their journey from Egypt to the Promised Land, they continually forgot the Lord's blessings and would complain, grumble, and groan. I have always thought they were crazy because they kept forgetting all the amazing miracles God was doing in their lives. He delivered them from Egypt, helped them cross the Red Sea, made bitter water clean; yet they kept searching for control.

We, too, often forget to notice all the miracles God is doing in our lives. True joy and satisfaction is trusting the Lord will determine our steps. May you and I learn to live in His presence, trust in His direction, and recognize the blessings in journeys He maps for us.

Lord Jesus, I trust You with my life. I give You my plans, desires, and dreams. Help me notice the blessings in my journey of life. I know You have the best plans, and I thank You for guiding me. Amen.

~**Mrs. Sanders, educator**

Focus

Then Peter called to him, "Lord, if it's really you, tell me to come to you, walking on the water. "Yes, come," Jesus said. So Peter went over the side of the boat and walked on the water toward Jesus. But when he saw the strong wind and the waves, he was terrified and began to sink. "Save me, Lord!" he shouted. Jesus immediately reached out and grabbed him. "You have so little faith," Jesus said. "Why did you doubt me?"

Matthew 14: 28-31, NLT

~

I once had a particularly high-spirited little boy in my preschool class. Daily he struggled to focus on the tasks at hand. One day in particular, he repeatedly made unsafe choices in the classroom and was constantly yelling at other children. I walked over to him and led him from the surrounding distractions. As I tried to investigate his reasoning for melting down, his eyes began to wander. I did not want to yell and be a hypocrite to the advice I was about to give. I gently held his face with both hands and said, "Look in my eyes." He immediately concentrated on my voice, agreed to try safer ways of reacting to further problems, wiped his tears, and went about his day.

> When our focus goes off our Creator, we sink.

Chaos in our setting can make chaos in our spirit. I have found myself raising my voice at my own children when things get out of control. It is not the reaction I want to give or that I want them to give to each other in the future, but it happens. I can just imagine God watching my home on a given chaotic day, trying to get my attention in any way possible. He sees my frustration. He hears my raised voice, just like I did with my student. I am sure He wants to gently hold my face and say the same words I uttered, "Look in My eyes." Everything else disappears when we focus on Him. We can concentrate on His voice, agree to try better ways of reacting to future stressful situations with His help, wipe our tears, and go about our day victoriously.

When our focus goes off our Creator, we sink. The good part is that when we call to Him and look in His eyes, he immediately grabs us from the depths. Our situations may not automatically change, but our perspective will. Shift your focus from your problems, failures, and frustrations to the eyes of your Creator and see how different your world becomes.

Jesus, I love You. In the midst of all the noise of life, help me always look in Your eyes for comfort and guidance. Keep my mind positive through the daily mundane tasks needing completed. They become more of a calling than a bother when my thinking aligns with Yours. Thank You for always lifting me back up. I praise You! In Jesus' Name.

~ Jennie Schueller, fourth-grade teacher

God Grows

I planted, Apollos watered, but God was causing the growth. So then neither the one who plants nor the one who waters is anything, but God who causes the growth.

I Corinthians 3:6-7, NASB

~

We are held accountable for how we perform the task.

"Why did he do that?" "What was she thinking?" "I taught them better than that!"

Well, maybe you did. Probably you did, and likely it will stick later when you do not expect it. As a teacher, I have one particular thing in common with you, the parent; we have both been given a role in training up a child in the way he or she should go. This can be frustrating at times and very rewarding at times. Regardless, it is always worth it.

Often we make this training process about us. So, we think that we will stop making it about us and focus on the trainees. That is wrong too. We need to make it about the Grower. Who is the one who actually causes the growth of a child? God is. We have a role, of course. We should do our best because we are held accountable for how we perform the task given to us. However, there is comfort when we remember that God causes the growth!

This comfort is important for two reasons. First, it is a safety net of sorts for when we mess up. We are all sinners: teachers, parents, students. All have sinned and fallen short (Romans 3:23). When the trainer messes up, there is comfort in knowing that God causes the growth of the trainee in spite of the trainer's errors. Second, this comfort is important because we have assurance that God can and will grow the student who currently has similarities to a wilted plant, parched for water. We need to remember that the Grower is also the One who created us out of nothing and will resurrect us in the future. We truly have access to Miracle Grow™!

How we cultivate and train does matter, but the growth is securely in the hand of the Master Gardener!

Dear Great Gardener, Please grow me how and when You want. Help me to cultivate as You want. Help me to put my trust in Your power to grow. May You grow what You want for Your glory!

~Six-year educator

Reaping Rewards

Do not be deceived: God cannot be mocked. A man reaps what he sows.
Whoever sows to please their flesh, from the flesh will reap destruction;
whoever sows to please the Spirit, from the Spirit will reap eternal life. . .
Let us not become weary in doing good, for at the proper time we will
reap a harvest if we do not give up. . . let us do good to all people.

Galatians 6:7a-10a, NIV

~

The apostle Paul encouraged believers to sow to the Spirit, not to the flesh, because the guaranteed consequences are radically opposite. Interestingly, people do not become weary in sowing to the flesh (selfishly doing only what they want to do). It seems that weariness comes when we deny ourselves for the sake of others or our own character. You can increase your score/level on "Call of Duty" or tutor a struggling student. Which is better for your character, shows concern for others, and pleases God more? Doing good is the cure for the selfishness that hinders your spiritual growth; you will be rewarded, if you do not give up.

> You will be rewarded, if you do not give up.

The plains of the wilderness are strewn with the bones of those who, at the moment of entering into Canaan (the blessing of God), simply gave up and never entered in.[14]

Heavenly Father, When I am weary and question the value of my efforts helping others, may I be reminded of my reward and refreshed by Your presence, so I will not give up. Amen.

~Dr. Thomas Reedy, Bible and English

Wait Patiently

I waited patiently for the LORD; he inclined to me and heard my cry.

Psalm 40:1, ESV

~

Waiting is a challenge for each and every one of us. Our society is turning into a fast-paced people; and when we want something, we want it now.

Let go of our control and let God do His thing!

Waiting patiently is even more of a challenge because now you have to wait without becoming anxious. This is a struggle as we tend to become irritated and irrational when we have to wait patiently. I have seen it in the grocery store, on the road driving, in church, in school, and even in the home. Sometimes we just want quick answers, and we will go out of our way to figure things out on our own. God has amazing plans for us if we will just exercise this fruit of the Spirit!

One of the greatest men in the Bible, David, had his patience tested. He asked the Lord many times if He would help him in battle or overtake a people group. Every time the Lord replied with an answer that would encourage David to wait because He had big plans for David if he would simply wait. He was very successful as king, and many people groups were delivered into his hands because he waited patiently. Imagine if David had not waited! There are many verses in 1st and 2nd Samuel telling us that the Lord was with David the entire way. He went from being a shepherd boy to a powerful and godly king! Imagine our lives if we let go of our control and let God do His thing!

Dear Lord, I want to thank You that we can be confident when approaching You. I am thankful that You hear my cries. I pray that You will give me strength to have self-control, to wait patiently on Your perfect plan and perfect time. You know my future and hold me in Your hands. I look forward to seeing what You have in store for me. I love You. Amen.

~ **Mrs. Bethany L., sixth-grade teacher and new mommy**

Forever Love

Love is patient…

I Corinthians 13:4a, NIV

~

Using Great Grandma's secret sugar cookie recipe, my mom and I were actively baking in the kitchen. Lots of ingredients, chilled dough, rolling, and cut outs later, it was time to bake them. I begged for the honor of slipping them into the oven. I excitedly carried the pan, slightly tipping it in order to slide it onto the shelf. Horror. In a split second, the cookies slid together, morphed into a lump, and rolled onto the floor. My heart dropped, knowing I had blown it. We had worked so hard, and I had dropped them. I slowly turned to look at my mom, fearing her disappointment and anger.

> The exercise of patience has great power to be eternal.

Instead, she sighed and then laughingly walked over to give me hug. She loved away my dismay. Her joy was contagious and all was well. I do not remember anything else about the day. But that moment, her exercised patience, has been encouraging me for forty years, reminding me to share the same grace with my own children.

Patience has unkind companions. It is yoked with inconvenience, loss, inadequacy, and failure. Though each trait strives to dominate the human mind, patience unleashed sweeps them all away.

As you consider your own family memories, which moments are the ones that will last forever? The exercise of patience has great power to be eternal.

Father, I acknowledge that You are always patient with me. Please allow my heart to reflect Yours as I deal with people around me. I want to shine kindness, patience, and love in every moment, no matter the stress. Amen.

~ Mrs. Gill, academic dean

Notes

1. Lewis, C.S. *Till we have faces.* Orlando, Florida: Harcourt, Inc; 1956, 1984.

2. Augustine. *Confessions.* Trans. Henry Chadwick. New York: Oxford University Press; 2008.

3. Batterson, Mark. *The circle maker.* Grand Rapids, Michigan: Zonderan; 2011.

4. Relationship. Religion. Merriam-Webster.com. Merriam-Webster. [Accessed 2013 May].

5. Ramsey, Dave. Dave Ramsey.Com "Baby Step 7." [Accessed 2015 April 12].

6. Yaroshenko, Mykola. *Life is everywhere.* Oil Painting. Public Domain.

7. Smallwood, Richard. Total Praise." Psalms, Hymns, & Spiritual Songs." CD. 2004.

8. Erma Bombeck. BrainyQuote.com, Xplore Inc, 2015. http://www.brainyquote.com/quotes/quotes/e/ermabombec106409.html [Accessed 2015 September 4].

9. Redman, Matt. "Blessed be Your Name." *Where Angels Fear to Tread.* CD. 2002.

10. MacDonald, Betty. "The Radish Cure." *Mrs. Piggle Wiggle.* New York, New York: Harper Collins Publishers. 1947.

11. Lyrics.net, STANDS4 LLC, 2015. "I See the Moon Lyrics." Accessed 2015 September 4.

12. Jobe, Kari. "The More I Seek You."

13. West, Matthew. " Forgiveness." *Into the Light.* CD. 2012.

14. Knowledge. Wisdom. Merriam-Webster.com. Merriam-Webster. [Accessed 2013 May].

15. Taylor, Jack. Quote taken from sermon notes taken in a conference in the 1980s.

Contributors

*Thank you so much to each of the following educators willing to submit their writing for the sole purpose of blessing families. Your time and creativity are valued and precious. May the Lord pour out His blessing for your sacrifice.***

@

Ambro, Donna

Anonymous

Bacon, Michelle

Beasley, Alethea

Bell, Brenton

Bluebaugh, Jacob

*Boll, Amy

Briseno, Layla

Casey, Melanie

*Coats, Sarah

Curtis, Lauren

*Drum, David

Eames, Donna

Esparza, Emir

Evans, Ryan

Finch, Greg

Flowers, Becky

Fourth-grade teacher
   & military wife

Gamber, Karen

Gill, Kimberlee

*Gill, Patrick

Gillespie, Andrea

Green, Verna

Hamline, Jennifer

Hardinger, Sarah

Harrelson, Linda

Holt, Kathy

Jurkovich, Jana

Kates, Ashley

*Kernsvaal, Vicki

L., Bethany

*Lawyer, Karen

LaFollette, Brittany

Lipps, Hannah

Lucht, Trissa

McEwen, Laura

*Merrell, Christy

Mickelson, Anthony

Musil, Mary

Mussatti, Anne

Nagy, Michelle

Patneau, Cheryl

Ray, Julie

Reed, Arlene

Reedy, Tom

Sanders, Charissa

Santon, Sue

*Satterfield, Chris

Schluben, Bob

Schmidt, Elizabeth

Schmidt, Judy

Schueller, Jennie

Seale, Kim

Shelton, Matt

Siemsen, Amber

Slagle, Lisa

Speaks, Megan

Stam, Emily

Stam, Wayne

Strange, Austin

Teilborg, Trish

Terry, Ruth

Utility Player

Velazquez, Ismarily

Wayman, Sheri

Welch, Kreg

Wilfong, Katelyn

* Denotes editing or
creative design
support

** The production of our devotional occurred over a period of years. Since that time, some of our beloved faculty have retired, moved to follow their next call, or passed away. We remain united in heart in encouraging parents to stand firm in their course to raise warriors for the kingdom of Christ. You can email us at <u>devotedparent@sca-kc.org</u>.